WHAT IS NOT

CAMELIA ELIAS

WHAT IS NOT

MARSEILLE TAROT À LA CARTE

EYECORNER PRESS

What is Not: Marseille Tarot à la Carte © Camelia Elias 2019
Published by EyeCorner Press in the series Divination Books
Cover design, silver gelatin print image, and typesetting by
Camelia Elias

ISBN: 978-87-92633-43-9
August 2019, Thy, Denmark

Images of cards:
Marseille Tarot by Jean Noblet, 1650
Reconstructed by Jean-Claude Flornoy
With kind permission by Roxanne Flornoy

All other images and photos are the author's own, featuring cards in private collection for which she has exclusive copyright

For Nisargadatta who said:
'You can come to me.'

CONTENTS

One action at a time / 9

Fundamentals in reading a visual text / 23
22 trumps according to the question / 43

When Justice is your full stop / 71
When the Charioteer is out of here / 79
When the Wheel of Fortune is not about plans / 83
When Force is on the dot / 89
When the World is not a cheat sheet / 95
When the Hermit is Eros / 101
When the Moon is not creative / 107
When the Lovers are ridiculous / 113
When the Magician doesn't improvise / 121
When Death is a deity / 128
When the Emperor lightens the heart / 133
When the Empress is disgruntled / 137
When the Sun needs no trust / 141

When the Popess ghostwrites / 147
When the Hanged Man can't help it / 157
When Temperance is obsessive / 165
When the Star does more than kneel / 169
When the Devil is crystal clear / 179
When the Tower is a tag / 183
When the Fool is an idiot / 189
When Judgment is about alternative history / 201
When the Pope is not arrogant / 207
The hands and the eyes / 215

Cited and selected works / 219

ONE ACTION AT A TIME

FIRST THE QUESTION. Then the shuffling. I shuffle the cards without thinking. 'Don't you think of the question while shuffling?' students often want to know. 'I don't,' I say. 'When I listen to the question, I listen to the question, and when I shuffle, I shuffle.' The notion that the diviner has to enter a special place beyond the mundane, where she can access divine or higher wisdom is quite foreign to me. What does it mean? Has anyone actually experienced that, going beyond the story level of identification: 'I, the diviner'?

When I shuffle the cards I concentrate. That's the only mental state I'm interested in entering. 'Yes, but isn't this equal to focusing on the question?' some still insist. 'No,' I say. 'What I'm focusing on is what I do, what my hands do, and how the cards move between my hands. I listen to the sound that my shuffling makes. I feel the texture of the cards. I check with my mind and what it resists. I reject plastic, and rejoice in linen. I catch myself reacting to what irritates me. Why do I cling to my preferences? Cotton cards are so much better than plastic... What's up with this judgment?

If I get this far into my thinking while shuffling, I'm already off the concentration path. My consciousness is moving, disclosing my weakness. I don't like weakness. I like vigilance. If I catch myself moving too much in the wrong direction, mentally and in my technique of laying down the cards, I make an effort to bring myself to what is the case. And the case is that I'm shuffling the cards, not doing something else. While the story of calling on ancestors, invoking my lucky star or the Devil, entertains me, I see it for what it is. A story, a mental image I bring to my consciousness, perhaps indeed, for a particular purpose. But what has it to do with shuffling itself?

I sink into my senses, and put the first card down. The Sun. Strike. I read for another. The second card is down. Strike. The World. It's where we're at, on the dot, in the middle of the circle. The third card is down. Strike. Force. The opening of the mouth.

I breathe out, and start the reading.

'This encounter you're having places you in a self-reliant position. What part of it provokes you? What is it that you don't like about it?'

'That people don't get it'.

'That's your fear speaking.'

'My fear?'

'Yes, your fear. You don't like losing ground. Being self-reliant is a state of groundlessness. When you rely on nothing and no one, there's no more ground to support you or to cling to. If you try to put your foot down, you'll step on fur. You'll be forcing what is not necessary. Put it down, your fear. Use your physical strength to understand the power of levitation. Don't look to another for support and validation. Find your own brilliant power to get what there's to get.'

'Oh, wow, that's a lot. Can I think about it?'

'Go ahead.'

READING CARDS FOR PRECISION

I grew up in communist Romania. This means that I grew up with a lot of competition: the math olympiad, gymnastics, the national championship for this or that. My school was practically visited by some selection committee almost on a monthly basis, though, on occasion, the committee was bigger and more important. Once the archery scouts were out. Very important people from Bucharest. The whole school had to be tested for natural abilities. I remember this one because I was the only student who got selected among 1100. I was 9. I was tiny and myopic. So what the hell was going on? Many asked that question, myself included. But sure enough, no one else had better precision in both firearm shooting and bow and arrow.

As far as I remember, there was a lot of commotion around the idea of selecting a tiny, myopic girl to train in Bucharest with the national champion team.

Mother opposed it, of course, for two reasons: 1) she was not interested in her daughter winning any Olympic competition in archery, and 2) the training was to take place at the other end of the country from where we lived. So that settled it, as it settled my ambition to become a champion at shooting – if I even had such an ambition. I don't remember that part.

I do return to this incident and memory, however, as it's only much later that I understood the motivation of the professional trainers. Of course they didn't care about my size or about my vision when they picked me for the national team, because it's neither size nor your eyes that does it. What does it is your breath. Ah…

In Japanese martial arts one talks about the concept of *hara*, which is to say, the condition you are in beneath your navel, three digits below, to be more precise. You're a champion already if you can breathe in such a way that you end up developing the power of your *hara*, as that is the power that wins whatever medals. The sports that require precision rely on techniques of exhaling, as the power to win is located at the end of the exhaling breath. I think that what my 9-year old self did when facing the target was to breathe in the bull's eye, and on exhale send the bullet and the arrow straight into it.

I didn't get to explore this further, as I never joined the archery team, but I did get to understand the principle behind breathing and its relation to shooting to precision when I started sitting in Zen meditation some years later. I also deepened my understanding of breath and its relation to clarity when I started instructing others in shooting to precision in academic and cartomantic settings. Working with the interpretative arts, Zen style, brought me to the insight that 'word and image' are the same.

You look at an image and words pop into your head. But whose words? What form do they have? What tone and color? The truth is that you can't decide. You don't know what's yours and what you invent based on convention, inspiration, or dictation. Getting around the constraints of your language is next to impossible, as this would presuppose an act of emptying yourself of all conceptual thought.

You're welcome to think, 'I'll be damned', because this 'damnation' is what I'm interested in exploring here, namely the idea that it *is* possible to look at images and take what we see inversely, or from the other end of what tradition prescribes.

I'll make this claim: just as size and eyes don't matter in sports that require hitting the bull's eye, but rather, correct breathing, so words, lists of random meanings and grand proclamations don't matter when you read your cards.

If you read your cards with a well-developed *hara* power, that is to say, the power of the gut that knows how to breathe and doesn't simply rely on some cliché notion of the intuitive faculty, then you get to experience what reading like the Devil is all about.

INHALE, EXHALE

Before I move on to saying something about why you're reading this book, and before you read further, I invite you to perform a short practice. Think of it as a practice that applies the *hara* power to your penetrating vision (even if you happen to be myopic). If you're not familiar with the Marseille cards, don't worry.

You'll be looking at images, not engage with stories about the significance of the individual cards.

Lay down three cards. Look at them as you breathe in. The vulnerability of this act – inhaling is a vulnerable act – will ensure that you perceive at the gut level all that which you don't want to hear. If your *hara* is strong, you can rest assured that your reading will not be an exercise in displaying anxiety, or in giving yourself what you want to hear.

Focus on the images of the three cards taken together without thinking *meaning,* for example the idea that Justice means truth, the Hanged Man means resignation, and the World means completion. If you want to shoot for precision, the last thing you want to do is activate a list of random Tarot meanings.

So, breathe in what you see with the condition you're in below the navel. That's the condition that will read the cards for you beyond your regular fear.

Exhale. Make it a long breath. Note the kind of power your breath has on the last bit, when there's no more movement. Now shoot for your answer. I bet it will have the quality of a very fine cut. When your reading has *hara* power, it makes everything appear upright and clear, with nothing but your own regulated breath standing between your sharpness and the target.

DECONSTRUCTED CARDS

Last year I started a series of short essays that I published in my column, *The Cartomancer,* on Patheos, in which I explored looking at the Marseille Tarot trumps from the point of view of serving them entirely deconstructed. That is to say, serving them in an original from, after a process of unsettling and dislodging their 'standard' meanings.

What you're reading here is an expanded form of the idea. Each of the 22 original essays has been reworked, now featuring also fresh and new readings of cards that have not been shared in the public space. The Zen nerve is also strong and nasty, showing no mercy.

Why deconstructed cards? Think: if we go mainstream, everything we're taught about the Tarot is in the form of method and an idea that adds to our notion of how we can think of the self in an amplified dimension. The archetype notion adds to the human character, making it bigger and better. Even your shadow is bigger than your conscious mind, and certainly better when you integrate it. 'Whoa,' people say, 'give me more.'

If we turn to the pip cards, the same subtle principle of addition is in place: The pip cards give you something, force, energy, love, the air that you breathe, or the symbolic power of money. 'Whoa,' people say, 'give me more.'

Throughout my time invested in studying cartomancy and practices of divination, I can safely say that not once did I come across the notion that it may be a good idea to think of subtraction. It's obvious to me that, all things being equal, if there's addition, then there's subtraction as well. Yet, while we have no problem locating where we add, it's more difficult with subtraction. 'Surely we can't rule out the shadow,' some would object, 'it has to stay in.' Fair enough. When we don't predict events with the cards, we like to contemplate on what we imagine is under the surface of our conscious minds and acts. The notion of the 'shadow' can prove useful, as it's instrumental in understanding another difficult idea, that of 'inner demons'.

However, we must think of divination as a means of working with images in such a way that we clearly see what the cards give us in terms of ideas, and what the cards suggest that we get rid of. In a reading with the cards it's good to have an eye on what is given and what is taken away, see when there's a call for piling up on the ideas, and when we must discard them or simplify.

Think of this concrete example that we might identify as a 'Justice card situation': 'You're so awesome, I recommend your work everywhere.' Love is given, you say thank you, and nothing else. Then the counter reaction. 'Why aren't you more human, see my needs and give me what I want, right now?' Love is taken away. A 'swords situation' sets in, overruling the balancing cups, and you're left wondering about the vampires of the world who give you love on condition that you now owe them, your blood to be more precise, or a pound of flesh, if we want to go Shakespearean.

The point is that when we recognize such situations, we can investigate the consequence of the mainstream idea that what the Tarot teaches us is mainly about giving and hardly ever about taking away. I'm interested in the latter, in subtraction and detachment, because any kind of boasting and unjustified hyperbolic speech provokes me, from marketing to identity shouts.

Look around: one simply cannot get big enough in business or in selfhood. One's problems must also be big, so that the solutions offered are equally big. Anything else is not 'inspirational.'

I don't read cards from this one-sided perspective. I don't set out to 'empower' my clients who seek my counsel. I read the cards and keep both giving and taking away in mind. I also activate a few useful mantras when presented with the temptation to deliver what's popular. Chief among them is, 'I don't think so.'

ABRACADABRA

In all my cartomantic teaching I point to the importance of detachment when reading cards, so that projection is minimized. But detachment as a principle is not something that you learn with the cards. You learn to detach when you're able to identify what language does to you, and what's being sold to you in so many words. What language is used in the delivery of the 'big,' and how prone are you to taking the words at face value?

If you understand how language operates, you understand what constitutes your feelings. You discover that you now intuitively know what the function of the Death card is followed by the Empress. It's not about the statement, 'more transforming power to you,' but the inverse of the situation. It's less. It's nothing. Can you say that to a woman who seeks to improve her predicament, that she's in for less, or, indeed, for nothing, or will you search your brain for the most current inspirational words to give, words that will make 'nothing' suddenly appear as 'everything?'

This kind of *abracadabra* is a magical act, but what I have to say about it is that it belongs to a different register. I don't operate with the 'transformational' and the 'alchemical' in my work with reading cards. I work with seeing things as they are. And it starts with knowing beforehand that language is a trap. I pay attention to its constructions and nothing but.

The images I'm looking at are also subject to language, as there's no 'silent' interpretation. If something falls into my head in the form of 'inexplicable' messages, I recognize instantly that what falls into my head are words, by definition fictions. Here, I consider my job as a diviner my ability to distinguish between the different types of fictions I'm dealing with, and select the most appropriate ones to the situation.

I read the cards from the perspective of what gives. When there's no giving, I say so. The condition, however, for saying so, or for 'saying it like it is' – a preferred line among diviners – is that you can actually distinguish between the layers of social constructions that we're all subject to. A reading predicated on fantasy, inspiration, validation, and endorsement, is not a reading like the Devil.

CARTOMANTIC FICTIONS

This book is not a historical study in the cartomantic dissemination of 'meanings' across traditions. In this book I follow my own sensibility and training. This means that what I have to offer is a philosophical rumination on the workings of language, as language informs the construction of visual images in context.

My general preoccupation is not with history, but rather with what we do with the cards in a divination setting, when we look at them and try to create a story via interpretation, deduction, language awareness, deconstruction, and the decoding of a visual text according to formal principles of design. For a more historically oriented take, I refer the reader to my essay in pamphlet form, *Divination with the Cards: A Short History,* first published for the online research archive, *Occult Studies* (2017).

In this book I use, however, the following terms that anchor my discussion in a historical perspective:

'Traditional Tarot' refers to classical fortunetelling and divination practices that are very much situationally based in a specific culture. There's no set 'history' for fortunetelling, as much of the original transmission of the cartomantic lore was oral. What we have in the genre of cartomancy are a few texts presenting conjectural knowledge, not fact.

As far as I'm concerned, anything pertaining to what we term 'personal gnosis,' or the transmission of knowledge via dreams or omens in the fortunetelling and grimoire tradition, falls under the category of fiction, not history. As I'm interested in literary texts, I see occult fictions as having the same value of orienting us in coping with the world as literature does.

Taking this aspect into consideration, I should then also mention that 'traditional Tarot' does not refer to the rise of the Tarot as an artifact in Italy around 1450.

The term 'esoteric Tarot' covers roughly the time spanning from the French occultism of 1760 to the British occultism of the Hermetic Order of the Golden Dawn.

ACTS OF REVISION

In this book I'm going to address the imbalance created by looking at the beliefs around the Tarot that we never question. I'll give 'awesomeness' – and along with it, bigness, the shadow, and the omnipotent – such a nice samurai sword blow, that it will never recover. I will shift the discourse from the plus to the minus.

The first chapter is an introduction to the fundamentals of reading a visual text. The chapter that follows looks at all the 22 trumps of the Marseille Tarot from the perspective of the question.

The remaining text is an investigation into how we can see the trumps of the Tarot addressing current issues, when the individual cards are not seen as representations of symbolic meaning, but rather as instances that highlight how we think of cultural functions in a context that we desire to deconstruct, or strip of its pre-conditioned setting. For instance, I'm interested in questioning to what extent the card of Death is not a better candidate for the notion of 'success' than its more standard counterparts, the Charioteer, or the Sun.

However, in my pointing out functions, I will not use the method of creating lists à la, 'the function of the Emperor is to rule.' I leave it up to the reader to put two and two together according to the nuances of each person's specific cultural contexts. A sharp reading arises out of that.

Finally, the book ends with a chapter on how to apply one of the concrete cartomantic principles to all your readings, the idea of looking at hands and eyes.

In my general narrative about the trumps of the Tarot I'm interested in developing a discourse around the trendy 'vulnerable story' as a plus, showing the detrimental aspect of having to rise to people's demands that 'you beg for it,' beg for mercy – you didn't mean to be too confident – beg for forgiveness – you didn't mean to speak the utter truth – and so on.

I find it odd that when we talk so much about empowerment, using the images of the Tarot for developing better awareness of our strength and weakness, we must resort to the false modesty that's called 'taking pride in full disclosure.'

In my work with the contemplative arts, I have as yet to see an actual interest from anyone in the story that has people go from rags to riches. Who cares, exactly? I insist on bringing to the reader's awareness this aspect of what we mean by 'empowerment,' as I see that there's a general tendency among diviners to mirror in their services cheap marketing tricks that have quite the opposite effect. If the premise for empowerment is to merely validate seekers in their quest, then what is offered is not divination, but a story that encourages identifications and the pursuit of embodying desired identities. All of zero value.

In my work, I see myself participating in the discourse that prioritizes reflection, analysis, and judgment over any type of emotional content. If an emotional core is touched, then I sincerely hope that it's the opposite of the 'feel-good about it,' whatever *it* may refer to. I find working with the Tarot cards a possibility to become more attuned to what we're saying and why, when we offer guidance or direct answers to questions, rather than stretching the figure of an archetype across the bar that's not even possible to jump over.

Therefore here, I simply propose that we start looking at the trump cards from the perspective of their capacity to participate in a discourse that dislodges the cliché expectation. What I stress in this book is direct experience. We look at the cards and understand that what we get from them is not the usable – something that most people expect from the so-called spiritual world – but rather, the usurp-able. Transacting only with finding things useful, and never usurping the false premise that often underlies 'the useful' and 'the relatable' is only half the story.

Let's look at the other half, the half that takes away the notion that we read cards because we want to get enlightened about our situation or the future. Perhaps we want to read cards for the simple reason that they enable us to say, 'I don't think so, it is not so', about what we think we want or we fear.

I myself read cards from a rigourous Zen perspective, one that allows for no belief or habitual thinking to get too comfortable in its seat. You will notice that even my writing will attempt to dislodge what you may expect, as I go in and out of inconsistency. For instance, some chapters are short and others are long, even though they share the same function and category. Some will also feature a whole series of basic principles right in the middle of a narrative that otherwise has an 'innocent' topic in focus.

While I want to say that, if you get through this whole book you'll see what's self-explanatory, I prefer to leave it entirely to your judgment to see what value there's in it, if there is any at all. In this sense, *What is Not* addresses both the young and the old, the inexperienced and the seasoned reader. Along the way, I also discuss the trappings of social media, as this is the space where most diviners make themselves visible. What do we buy in terms of knowledge and wisdom, and how we do sell ours? It is my deliberate choice to put people on the spot, as any deconstructive project can do nothing but. I adopt the offensive tradition passed down to me from true masters of language and desire, from Zen monks to nonduality radicals and fortunetellers of caliber.

In this book, I only offer examples of reading the Marseille Tarot trumps.[1] The reading of the 3-card string is also the most frequent, though 4 and 5-card spreads will also occur. In doing so, my emphasis is on training the reader to see the functions of the cards as they relate to a context that they can deconstruct, before awareness of how the cards apply to the very situation also sets in. My desire is to elicit this response: 'Aha, indeed, why not see the cards also like this, as it makes perfect sense.'

If I achieve this aim, then I declare this book a great success.

---

1 For work on how to read the pip cards, that is to say, reading with the full Marseille Tarot deck, I refer you to my book, *The Power of the Pips: Courting Numbers in Cartomancy* (2017).

FUNDAMENTALS IN READING A VISUAL TEXT

STRONG STRUCTURE, bold statement, clear line, and yes or no. A good divination session is about form, not content. A good divination session is about identifying first what is precisely *not* the case, before you pass judgment on what *is* the case. Let's see what I mean.

In my cartomancy teachings I don't teach lists of meanings. I don't do it simply because I prefer to think about what catches my eye when I look at a picture. I start with this question: what's interesting here? How does this work? – and by this I mean, how does composition work? A good visual composition grabs you by the heart and is unforgettable.

So with the divination act that is very much a mirror of the visual text in front of you. That is to say, a good divination session with the cards is unforgettable because reading the images right hits the nerve that responds to what is obvious to the unconscious mind. The conscious mind responds to clichés because it's safe, because it learned what is culturally appropriate – everyone weeps at a wedding – but the unconscious mind responds to truth, taboo, and bold statements. Imagine a wedding ceremony that's beyond the cliché. I haven't seen one yet, for all the planning and the formal preparation that goes into it...

THE STRONG STRUCTURE

Although all divination with the cards is an interpretative art, the skill that goes into it is no different than what we do when we perform a picture analysis, when we know unambiguously why an image works and why another doesn't. Why do some pictures come across flat and boring? Why are others dynamic, full of depth and contrast, and thus able to grab your heart?

A good visual text is good simply because it has a solid structure. A solid structure is not 'many things,' nor is it 'all over the place.' When you look at the cards that present you with symmetrical duos and trios, what you respond to is not the cliché: 'Here's the Devil and here's the Pope, each performing their devilish and dogmatic duty; that means something.' What you respond to is a correlation factor that's anchored in a clearly recognizable cultural context.

If you say to someone, 'first the wedding and then hell' – upon seeing the cards of the Pope first and then the Devil – what you're pointing to is not an inherent meaning that the cards supposedly possess, but rather, a situational positioning. Culturally speaking, it's better to be blessed by the Pope than cursed by the Devil.

The latter can seem attractive to some, but it will never work in a culturally consecrated context. Try telling everybody that the Devil officiated at your wedding ceremony, and see how far you get with acceptance. The Wiccans in the 60s and 70s notoriously did that, but all they achieved was a whole lot of noise and newspaper headlines that ultimately led to divorce; divorce from society followed by internal strife. A lot of devotees would later split with their covens, the Devil, the high priests, and the drama, retiring also from the general public eye.

Some graphically explicit stories make it into a text, contributing to the creation of great literature. But just as is the case with images, what makes a literary text good is not the fluff and the amount of descriptive detail that goes into it. Rather, what makes a literary text good is a solid structure and a bold outline that makes an unambiguous statement. Even poetry that operates with a highly ambiguous content must hit the nerve of the obvious if it's to succeed. If it's merely ambiguous, poetry falls into forgetfulness faster than your scrolling on the internet.

As a literature professor I used to teach students about how to look for the strong statement at both the visual and verbal level in a text. As a cartomancy teacher I do the same. I say, 'look at this picture or a string of pictures together and ask yourself why it works, why it enables you to say bold things, unheard of things, and things of substance that touch the heart.' The answer, 'it works because it worked for other diviners in the past and I'm working within that lineage' is not a good answer. An answer like that relies on imitation, on rendering a flat image of what is otherwise plain and obvious, staring you in the face.

I've written plenty about what divination is *not* about, and why I associate my practice with the discipline of paying attention, calling what I perform *martial arts cartomancy*[1]. But here I want to insist on truncating it even more. So let's look at a few fundamental principles again, associated with the method of reading like the Devil.

IT'S NOT ABOUT LISTS AND DECKS

It's not about what set of cards you use: 'This is modern, this is antiquated, this is cool, this is art, this is occult, this is witchy, this is esoteric, this is literal, this is fortunetelling, this is Marseille, this is Rider Waite.' It's about giving even the most trivial of questions a strong backbone and structure. What goes for life, goes for reading cards: Form, balance, boldness, and uniqueness.

Lists of meanings, or charts and correspondences have nothing to do with a sitter's hopes and fears, but everything to do with the reader's hopes and fears. Are you beyond yours yet? If not, ask yourself why. How are you going to be bold, unique, balanced, and nuanced in your readings, if you're fearful of how the other you read the cards for may respond, or if you're hopeful that what you say is relatable?

Marketing and commerce works with exploiting people's hopes and fears. What you're doing is divine for that which is beyond the cliché. Lists of meanings may seem like a treasured

---

[1] See my edited collection of short essays, *21+1 Fortune-teller's Rules: Read like the Devil manifestoes* (2018).

vault or safety-net, but all they ever do is lock you in the world of clichés.

Sometimes I think about writing a straight book of meanings based on the scribbling that other diviners before me did on the backs of their cards. I have many old decks that feature both borrowed meanings and personal wisdom, duly handwritten on the back of each card. If I wrote that book, I could at least claim that my sources are solid and beyond any further speculation or reproach.

Look at this old Etteilla inspired deck from the late 1800s. I got it solely because of the ink and the quirky handwriting on the cards. As to the rendered meanings, let us not even go there, as it's all flat, flat, flat, cliché after cliché. I prefer to think of this diviner being smarter than her own scribbling, and offering advice in accordance with seeing what's appropriate for each individual situation, that is, seeing the obvious under her nose, rather than going with what others before her have decided is the case.

As far as I'm concerned, if I can't explain to myself why the presence of three queens in a string of cards on the table means trouble, then all I ever do is repeat what is potentially ridiculous at the level of common sense.

Rarely, if ever, do the books that promise to uncover some secret meanings tell you where what is taken for granted comes from, that is to say, what rationale informs the charts and categories. I can imagine why three women together can lead to gossip, and hence trouble, and I can also understand why three women together is potentially worse than the situation when only two are together, ping-pong'ing their own experiences to one another and forgetting about third party issues.

But I will have a very hard time explaining it to myself why coins relate to the bones and the swords to the air. Is it because we tend to stash the coins inside our skin, as it were, and we wield the swords in the air?

I can think of a certain holy cup that's been hidden from sight – though some templars are now revealing the secret that what we call the holy grail has been staring us in the face – 'it's Mary Magdalene herself' – or an inscription tomb in England or Normandy, depending on who you're asking. As for the swords cutting through the air, why is that so special? Weren't batons trees once, growing tall and cutting through the air too?

My question to you is this: is the knowledge that lacks explanatory depth good knowledge?

The illusion of knowledge is worse than ignorance, which means that getting the fundamentals straight and leaning on a solid structure of seeing is not only desirable but ultimately obligatory.

IT'S NOT ABOUT THE SITTER'S PROBLEM

It's not about the subject either, or what a sitter puts on your table in terms of hopes and fears or concerns. It's about distinguishing between the shades of grey. What's essential in her question and what is not? Can you see the underlying structure of what a person is asking? Some pose very involved questions that don't even have anything to do with what they present as a problem. How do you rise to what you actually know in what you're doing, remembering also that staying uninvolved and detached is where compassion and clarity reside?

It's not sure that the sitter is clear in her own head about her issues. If she was, she wouldn't be sitting with you. The sitter is there to create a structure around your divination. She may have a story of her own life to tell, but getting that story is not the purpose of divination. The sitter comes to you for *your* story of the structure that she gives you. What might look like a lost love story is really only interesting because, looked at from another angle, it may easily turn out to be about winning a ticket to a grand cruise through paradise. First the truth, then the wedding...

The actual subject of a life-story is as meaningless as the lists of meanings that you find even in the best fortunetelling book. What's meaningful is the way in which you look at the underlying structure of what's being put on your table. How bold is the outline? A reader who possesses clarity is able to see more than 'emerging patterns.' She can see the obvious.

The structure of your divination must be bold enough and plenty astonishing, as that's the only way in which you can grab the sitter's attention on all levels, beginning with the heart, the conscious and the unconscious, and all the ensuing 'ahs' and 'ohs'. If the structure of your divination is not obvious beyond the cliché, the sitter won't go home with a memorable impression.

IT'S NOT FLEXIBLE MULTIPLE CHOICE

It's either this or that. Either he still loves her or he doesn't. Anything else in between is already using too many words. Too many words destroy the obvious. Too many words give the sitter an excuse to get distracted from the strong message. Why would you let her leave your parlor with a weak message? Because it's safer? Safer for whom?

Your sharp cut must be in the sitter's face. You don't negotiate with the punch line. You either laugh or you cry. You don't sit there with an unfinished story. 'But the Lovers card means love, or choosing what I love…' No, it doesn't. What determines the meaning of a card is comprised by what you want to know. *Why* you want to know it lends dynamics to this meaning.

Look at this string of cards:

If the Tower follows the Charioteer and we have the card of Judgment in the last position, it doesn't necessarily mean that the situation will improve, that you rise again to a new experience. When you crash, you crash. There's an announcement about it. That's the obvious. What's not obvious at all is the wishful thinking that goes into it. Maybe, just maybe the ones at the cemetery sharing the grave can collectively give you a push from the hereafter, but does being pushed mean an improved situation?

How often do you tell your sitters, upon seeing Judgment following the Tower or some other nasty card, that 'the situation will improve'? How do you know that? In olden times being lucky simply meant having power. When you're crushed you don't have any power. You're at the mercy. It's this mercy that determines where you're going, or where your sitter is going, not your illusion of control. Admitting that you're subject to conditions beyond your luck is more empowering than self-empowerment via a strong wish for power that you don't have. Pass that on to your sitter, and watch her reaction.

FORMALIST ART

To sum up here, divination is about paying attention to form, elements such as balance, tension, color, lines, light, speed, space, agency, and function.

You can have access to the collective wisdom and repository of knowledge of the diviners that came before you, or the ones you compete with, but having access doesn't automatically mean that you actually know yourself what you're talking about. The only way in which you can know that is if you take the time it takes to look at the structure that three or more cards together forms, so you can understand it beyond the illusion of knowing, beyond cliché and good memory.

If you want your readings raised to the power of art, then make an effort to understand the basic principles that constitute the formal composition of a divination session – from the question to the visuals of the image, including what the gestures and the body language of the sitter tell you. Or decide that, on occasion, you might actually want to take a break from reading books of meanings, and pick up instead books of fundamentals. Thank you for getting this one.

PEDAGOGICS OF 'I DON'T THINK SO'

We're not done with the proposition that a good divination session is all about form. Let's place what I had to say above in some sort of context, one of relatability, since making things relatable is the backbone of divination and many other venerable businesses. But we'll give it a twist.

As a Zen inclined person I don't dig duality. What is love and what is hate? They're both emotions of the same kind, of the same mind-set, of the same fiction.

From a linguistic point of view, duality is mightily entertaining. It's the drive behind all transactions. You don't behave properly, you'll go to hell instead of heaven. You have to love devotion to an idea, even when you hate it that the idea is all about prohibition. You want a powerful religion, you've got it right there, in the manipulation with opposites.

'I've been poor and I've been rich. It's better to be rich,' said famed writer Gertrude Stein, and we get the mechanism for desire right there.

'I'd love to have love in my life, more money, better health and a dream job,' we all say, giving in to the idea of what we imagine the good life is. We tend to hate what we have already.

'The Danes are the happiest,' the world thinks, and we presume that it has to do with economical reasons. While it's true that socialism works here, thank god for it, it's also true that the 'happy' people rather hate it, most of them being invested in the hunt for 'this is mine.' I live in Denmark. I can tell you about just how happy territorial people are.

The idea that I have something that you don't is also a successful premise for most businesses, from selling a fridge to selling reverse psychology, as in, 'no, it's not you who is creating all this drama, it's your shadow that does it.' I get a slew of emails every day from well-intended people who take it upon themselves to inform me that if I can't give myself permission to love myself, my shadow included, or rather, especially my shadow, they will give me this permission. Gracefully.

'But, but, wait a minute,' I want to say, 'what do you actually know about me?' I hear the silent answer at the other end: 'I know that you desire, and that's enough for my business.'

Right.

So, how does a Zen inclined person who writes and teaches cartomancy deal with all this?

She doesn't. Well, there's a dealing with it, but not in any obviously expected way. Let's see what I mean by giving you three points:

1. *There's the laughter.* When people go, 'you're like this, or like that' and then offer a counter solution to my identity problem, I laugh.

2. There's the question. When people go, 'your sticky patterns must be broken, and I have just the recipe for how you do it,' I ask, 'really?'

3. There's non-belief. When people go, 'I can save you, trust me, all you need to do is believe me when I tell you that this means something,' I go, 'I don't think so.'

99.9 percent of all businesses are anchored in the conceit that's called the savior syndrome. 'This brand new fridge saves you from food-poisoning.' 'Jesus saves you from all your sins.' 'Lucifer saves you from deadly boredom.' 'Magic saves you from conformity.' 'Bigness saves you from smallness.'

'Haha. Really? I don't think so.' That's what I say. I say all this because my assessment and evaluation of what's happening is entirely based on formal discernment. This is another way of saying that I pay attention to the underlying structure of the promises that are offered to me. What is this structure made of? My own desire as manipulated by the other, or an actual foundation I can build on?

When we read a visual text, a similar approach is needed simply because what we're up against is two things: 1) recognizing the symbolic value that's culturally attributed to the function of things – for instance, most people understand that the function of an emperor is to rule and command – and 2) recognizing the fact that symbols operate with shifting signifiers – for instance, a fool can represent both an idiot and an idiot savant. In other words, the idea that the Emperor in the Tarot 'means' power is only true half of the time, or else it's only true until it's not true anymore. The same applies to the Fool. He is a general nuisance until we get to see, depending on the context, the default wisdom that comes with non-attachment.

As meaning is situational, not fixed in stone, what the diviner thus needs when assessing the form and nature of a question is to cut right to the chase, using her own personal and sharp sword.

What does this mean? This means that you read the cards like no one else. There's no catalogue of meanings to save you. There's no empathy to save you. There's no compassion to save you. There's no second-thought to save you. There's no approved of drama queen to save you. There's no knowledge to save you. There's no history to save you. There's no claim whatsoever to save you.

There's only you and your ability to cut through it. Either you see what needs cutting, or you don't. Do the cards give you 'permission' to go beyond culture, to read a symbolic manifestation against its grain? I asked the cards to tell me.

The cards, the Sun, Force, and the Tower, said: 'two validate one another. If you have to go beyond culture, you must grab the other by his throat, asking: what is it exactly that you believe in? Man-made constructions? To what end?'

The way forward is not an institution that others build in the name of this or that Babel Tower pretense. Cutting to the chase starts with dismantling, with a simple response: 'Haha, really, I don't think so,' whenever what is not actually the case is on the table.

DRAW, CUT, AND SHEATHE

Let me end this idea of the importance of form with a story that I've shared elsewhere, a story about the samurai culture, the culture that I find closest to my approach of reading the cards.

I could write a whole book about the art of fencing. Suffice it to say here that there's a school in the Japanese samurai tradition that's associated with the name of 'The Sword of No-Abiding'[2].

The truncated version is this: you're truly skilled and can avoid dying from another sword and in your own bed, if you can so master your mental swordsmanship that you never even have to draw the blade once in your entire life. The opponent only has to glance at you once, before he runs away screaming. How very excellent. How is that for a Zen paradox? It's a good one.

Now, one of the countless representations of this fascinating school is in popular culture. Film, to be more exact. I watch a lot of those, in translation, alas. I watch samurai films every night, and on occasion also in the morning with my coffee. Like today, for instance. I don't even care if the films are good or bad – though I prefer those from the 60s. What interests me is the sword and the silk. The swooshing of the silk against the blade... I possess both, silk and swords, but not all from the period.

---

2 See the book *Zen and Japanese Culture* by Daisetz Suzuki (1959).

I have many favorite Japanese actors, but I find Raizô Ichikawa intriguing. He knew how to play 'faces' and 'masks.' A sublime actor who died at 37. I'm still in mourning.

But let me get to the point and link this to cartomancy.

In the film *Ken Ki* from 1965, (*Diabolic Sword*) Hanpei (played by Raizô Ichikawa) is an orphan who is terribly mobbed, but manages to become a florist at the court.

One day in the woods to collect soil for his flowers he meets a Ronin, an unattached Samurai practicing his art. He is amazed at the man's precision to cut a butterfly into three parts with one move.

He asks: 'What is this sword style, sir, and how can I master it?'

The samurai says: 'It's very simple. Quickly draw your sword, cut, and put it back. That's all.'

Hanpei is most impressed but also discouraged. He can claim no training at all in any swordsmanship.

The Samurai explains: 'There's a big difference between *kenjitsu* and *iai* (fast draw). In *kenjitsu* there are a lot of untrue techniques behind it. But in *iai* there's only one truth: Draw your sword, cut, and put it back. That all. If you want to master it, you have to see it with your own eyes. I won't teach you. Learn with your eyes, that's the essential thing.'

The next thing that happens is Hanpei's dedication. He goes to the woods every day to watch the master practice. After one year, the Samurai says to him: 'Now you've learnt everything.'

Hanpei is incredulous. He never touched a sword yet. 'Yes, master,' he says, I've now seen your technique and it's beautiful: Draw, cut, and sheathe. But that's all I've done, watch'.

The master goes: 'That's it. It's perfect.'

He gives Hanpei his sword with a glowing face. He is happy to have passed on his teaching before he died.

Now Hanpei is the holder of the style of 'draw, cut, and sheathe'. Invincible, he honors it to the end.

Now think: How do you read your cards like the Devil, which is another way of saying that you pay attention to form? Draw, cut, and sheathe. Draw the cards, cut the message to one line, and put the cards back into their pouch.

Again, draw, cut it as fast as you can to the essentials – you have been practicing just looking at the cards – for one year is good – and then put them back into their pouch. The condition for maintaining this high standard is the hard work that you put into watching. You watch and you watch and you watch. Repetition is the mother of achieving and maintaining mastery.

Watch the masters, whether the cards themselves are the masters, or someone else. It doesn't matter who, because they can't teach you what they do. But if they're free of all the 'untrue techniques behind it,' you can trust them to pass on to you something very special. But you still have to do it. Every day. Watch the cards. Patiently. You don't have to kill it immediately. You can try, but don't be so certain of your victory. There's always a meaner fortuneteller out there who can kill it much better than you do. What of your confidence then? Draw, cut, and sheathe. That's the secret. Now watch.

THE THING ITSELF

Reading cards is fascinating simply because their visual language enables us to bypass everything we know, or think we know. We often feel the need to explain our situation and condition. This is not possible without attachment to words, cultural context, and our relationship to both words and context. There are the cards, and then there are the stories about the cards.

If we just look at the cards without the need to understand anything, we arrive at the clarity that makes us realize that there's no knowledge that's not anchored in stories, in fiction, and symbolic relations.

I mentioned the Emperor. Let's look at the Empress too.

I can say, 'the Empress is like Venus, a goddess of love and money.' I can also say, 'the Empress is like the earth mother, nurturing and fertile.' And I can also say, 'the Empress is a calculated boss who's on top of everything.' What is all this? Stories. Which one is correct? One of them, all of them, or none of them?

Stories have a correlation to the imagination. But the imagination is the product of the mind. If you want the thing itself, not the story about the thing, then what?

When I look at these cards above I can say this: 'the Empress is the Empress, the Hermit is the Hermit, and the Moon is the Moon.' This would be an actual reading of the cards according to the cultural designations of the images I'm looking at.

In making such statements, what I also implicitly do is acknowledge functions. Each performs their job: the Empress sits on a throne and commands, the Hermit is searching, and the Moon goes from shining brightly to being dark.

If I leave it there, to identifying functions, I have a first-hand experience of the cards. If I say, 'the Hermit is a philosopher who's tired of the world, and renouncing it, he retreats to the mountain to get rid of his mind,' I'm creating a myth.

Granted, this is the advanced symbolic version and a little different than the one you find in the standard 'little white book' about the Tarot that comes with almost any standard tarot deck, one that associates the Hermit with spiritual attainment, inner life, wisdom, or the unveiling of secrets.

We talk about many cartomantic schools and traditions, but the main difference between them lies in this distinction: You either look at the primary function that the figures on the 22 trump cards or the 4 suits represent, or you look at the individual stories about the cards that people have contributed throughout the ages – some more interesting than others.

Granted again, everything is a story. When I say, 'the Empress is the Empress,' desiring to prioritize the job that the Empress performs rather than what she is, what I do is point to an embedded story already. But I like to think that it's a simpler story, a story that's stripped of embellished and made-up symbolic content, and as such, it's a story that's closer to clear insight.

Reading cards is fascinating because cards remind us of our job. How clear are you on what your job is? If you have to explain your situation and condition all the time, you're not clear on what your job is. The cards help us understand what a situation is, and how we can relate to it according to our function determined by the situation. The condition for gaining insight is that we bring a real question to the cards. Without a question, we just make things up. In other words, we read cards because they clarify for us the positions we have available to us. They spell out for us what kind of power we have to act in a given situation, showing us also the consequences of acting outside of our situation and function. Being able to cut it to the bones is not a small thing. That's why I call this kind of cartomancy 'martial arts cartomancy,' because it's anchored in understanding less and seeing more. It's a paradox that the more people 'understand' their condition and situation, the less they see the thing itself.

Reading like the Devil is like wielding a samurai sword. It's like saying: 'off with their heads, the heads of myth and story, so that the obvious can emerge.' Thus when I say, 'read your cards so you can see the thing itself, not have second-hand experiences of the thing,' what I say is this: see what you see, not what you desire to see. See what you do, like paying attention, not what you imagine that you do, like following endorsements. Watch the masters for a while, and then do your own thing, free of impressions and impersonations.

Mastering reading a string of three cards according to form and function is what gives you power over context and shifting symbols. Best of all is the ultimate question: 'What happened to my feelings? I have no feelings anymore. I don't fear that what I have to say is not correct. I need to trust no one for it, including myself. All I'm doing is seeing clearly.' Indeed, what has clarity to do with the theatricality classically associated with the job of the diviner? Draw, cut, and sheathe. Read the damn cards. There's just the theater you need in that alone.

In what follows we're going through the reading of a three card string that features each of the 22 trumps in context. In terms of subject matter, we'll keep it close to the most current and mundane issues. What are we plagued by, and how do we respond, especially when deconstructing a habitual response is what we're after? What is *not* the case, precisely, when we use the images of the Tarot that we have become accustomed to seeing in a certain symbolic way? What if we consider the function of the trumps first, before we think of grand archetype intangibles? What if the Emperor is just a well-dressed man sitting confidently, before he 'means' masculine principle, power, dominance, or any of the other standard Tarot terms that lack specific grounding?

22 TRUMPS ACCORDING TO THE QUESTION

I ALWAYS THOUGHT that straight fortunetelling is all about deduction, coupled with insight about the human condition, when the human condition designates suffering. How do people navigate suffering? You put the cards down, and you read them according to people's predicament. A predicament cannot be formulated without an implicit question. If the question is explicit, all the better, for the answer will be precise and on target.

I never read without a question simply because a reading without a question produces generalities. Generalities don't move me. I already also know that a general statement about a predicament doesn't move the other I read for either.

'What is a good question?' some always ask, and I always have various things to offer myself in terms of an answer. But since we're with a book about what is essentially a good idea to think of, question, and deconstruct against the grain of any dictation, my basic answer to the question, 'what is a good question?' is this: any question is a good question. Since the cards have endless ways of suggesting an answer, what we make of this answer is a matter of modulation, contrast, and levity.

I often hear in the cartomantic circles that not all questions are good, serious, ethical, or eliciting insight. This is all nonsense, of course, insofar as what we're dealing with here is a pack of cards that has no discrimination of its own. You pose any question to the cards, and the cards will give you an answer befitting your interpretative skills. In this sense the cards are far more democratic than the dogmatists populating the earth.

For instance, I don't see the usefulness of this claim: 'A bad question is, does he love me?' formulated by many opinion makers, especially in the social media. What is actually useful is what I do with the cards when I answer such a question. How do I go about it? How nuanced or modulated can I make my answer? Do I levitate the person I read the cards for with what I have to say, as in, do I raise their own level of distinction, or am I invested in adopting an unjustified righteous position, judging the question and questioning the motive for asking it? If I'm able to pay attention to the cards on the table, and see what there's to see, I fail to comprehend how my clarity about that can ever be deemed stupid, even if the question falls in categories that are not deemed kosher by the ones who have strong opinions about what is appropriate or not when reading the cards. My own opinion here is for everyone to mind their business and just read the damn cards.

With this in mind, let's do something original here. Let's look at the 22 trumps, and instead of describing them according to the mainstream rule of 'this means that,' let us imagine that they provide us with ample information for how we may think up a question, one that springs from what we can identify at the level of form and function. This exercise has the purpose of training your ability to see how each image contains a question within it already, and because of that, it lends itself to the precise answer.

We'll also look at how we can think of the trumps as carrying significance according to the question, and how that significance leads to the interpretation of the image via deduction.

THE MAGICIAN

In a question about *capacity,* the Magician suggests that you're not as capable as you think. You may be very skillful at a trick, but being good at waving your arms about does not equal capacity. 'Fake it till you make it' does not mean that you actually know what you're doing. If this card presents itself to you, ask yourself why you con yourself and others, and whether it's all worth it, especially if the Moon is also present. The last thing you want in the world, if you're into navigating through your suffering, is to project 'skills' and 'capability' in the form of shallow thinking.

THE POPESS

In a question about *inclination,* the Popess suggests that you be curious. Read. Read everything. Without inspiration from books, images, and reading other people (though, withhold judgement when reading others), there's no way you're going to know what you're inclined towards. All questions about 'finding your path' and following direction begin with an act of reading. Without polishing your vocabulary, there's no focus.

THE EMPRESS

In a question about *purpose,* the Empress suggests that you get the power if you get the man. Yes, I know, it's not fair. Culturally speaking, while the Emperor is thought of as the sovereign, the Empress is thought of as the consort. We can resist this nonsense, of course, and try to change this symbolic order of things, but if you want quick results, pay attention to what happens when you shift your focus from the Empress as an independent woman, and see her instead as a person who exercises her power via her husband and children. I bet you'll get more out of it, especially if the Sun is also in the picture.

THE EMPEROR

In a question about *strategy,* the Emperor suggests that what it takes to win is knowing what battlefield you're on. Is it open, closed, hot or cold, the war you're at? 'In times of peace, you think of war,' the sages of old had it, and they are right. The Emperor doesn't merely sit on a throne. His most active power is actually guarding; guarding the throne, the castle, and his territory. Rulership takes this vigilant guarding into account.

Think of it too next time you see the Emperor and want to get excited about your sovereignty. You pay a price for it that's not always the most attractive. The only good news is that strategizing is a lot of fun, when you're good at it, but being good at it presupposes a very keen sense of knowing your place. Yes, yes, you are the ruler, but precisely therefore, what you must know at all times is *why* and *how* you rule. Just being the ruler won't cut it. What makes a good ruler is knowing your place and correct timing for every act. Without these two, you're merely a fool thinking he has power. Beware of the Emperor next to the Fool.

THE POPE

In a question about meeting the *significant other,* the Pope suggests that you can rejoice. It's in the picture, your marriage. You'll get the blessing. When that is said, and considering the Pope's rather indifferent gesture, not really looking at the two kneeling before him, think of the idea of a disengaged person performing the counsel. I can't help thinking of the Pope thinking, 'it's just a bloody job.' How cynical, but such an at-  titude exists. My point is that you should not expect with the Pope's blessing the idea that it will last forever. In a predictive reading of the cards, when you break the news to them that they're going to get married, some think, 'oh, what a relief, I'm wanted in the respectable way', fallaciously anticipating the grand 'forever happy.' If giving his blessing is just a job for the

Pope, you can think of the same when you seek his counsel in connection with your idea of divorce some time down the road. The Pope won't endorse it as such, for he's after all a man of the church and there's a tradition for keeping a record of what you own. Namely, via marriage, the man owns the woman and the woman owns the man, that is to say, if both parties are in for symmetrical relations, which is not always a given, given that more often than not, there are more men than women who exert entitlement over and ownership of their partners.

If the Pope is next to Justice, then we can deduce via the function of these cards that we're here in the presence of 'the right one for you.' But I wouldn't lose sight of Justice being a representative of the court, where divorce battles are lost and won.

THE LOVERS

In a question about *doing what you like*, the Lovers card suggests the agony of love. Most get excited when seeing this card, but as far as I can see, an agony is an agony and therefore quite removed from bliss. It's not that you don't know which one to choose, but that you don't know what's culturally appropriate. And yes, we do want to talk about a young man's anxiety about what's culturally appropriate, because it exists.

I have as yet to meet young persons who even have the slightest clue about doing what they like. What would that be? Who is to determine it? Let us not confuse being under cultural pressure with the knowledge that you're now free to fuck, especially if you've reached a certain age.

The Lovers card is not about fucking, even if it may appear to be so. It's about anxiety and how to avoid being fucked by circumstance. Many a young man I know have gone for the woman who acts as a front, who comes across as respectable, successful, willing to breed children, and care for the house. Oh wow, that's so exciting, isn't it? When doing what you like is equal to playing for the gallery, playing it safe, then I don't know.

On my part, I steer away from the ambivalent types. If the Judgment card is also in the picture, then I know already what the deal is all about, namely, about being loud and showing off: 'Not only one, but two women are interested.' How unbecoming.

THE CHARIOTEER

In a question about *drive,* whether literal or Freudian, the Charioteer suggests momentum: 'Now is the time. Go for it.' The only thing you might wish to consider is your speed, especially if the Tower card is in the picture. Crashing is not a good idea, unless you do it on purpose and for show. Normally you would think that the Charioteer discloses knowing where you're going, but don't be so sure. Some drive in their cars for the sheer pleasure of it, though doing it to just enjoy nature and the sights is less and less common. No one has the time for such 'trivial' pursuits. Society says, your drive has to have purpose, it has to go somewhere.

Granted, having a goal may be a good idea, especially if you're duly submitting to cultural constraints that dictate: 'You must have a purpose, and not only that, but you must also demonstrate how you're going about achieving your goal.' Culture is so tedious in its demands, and we give in, but is stating a purpose the same as actually having one? How many people you know have a purpose that they've arrived at through self-reflection? I can only name a few Zen masters who fall into that category. The rest, well, let's just say that most drive around showing off their cars, and thinking that the fancy vehicle equals power, speed, motivation, clear direction, and arrival. Sigh... if only...

JUSTICE

In a question about *choice,* Justice suggests that whatever you go for, it's the right thing for you. I bet you thought that the card for choice is the Lovers. Well, think again. When Justice appears, we're with the idea that righteousness is not only something that nasty politicians profess. I live in Denmark. The most fascist oriented parties invoke 'just cause' in their propaganda. I want to pull my hair. What 'just cause?' Since when is the color of skin a dividing line for what is just and proper?

Justice as a virtue is about seeing things as they are, not about seeing things as you fancy to see them. Think of that next time you see Justice in the picture. If she's with the Pope, consider getting that marriage counseling done. If she's with the Tower, say goodbye to your husband. Your possessions will stay with you, and if the Emperor is in the picture, he might even let you have the house.

THE HERMIT

In a question about *making a difference,* the Hermit suggests that you can forget about it. What difference? What's up with this illusion? Culturally speaking, you don't even have to hit the 40s, before you realize that 'work' is overrated. But since you didn't bother to save up when you were in your 20s and 30s, you have to keep at it. Who's going to pay your bills?

When the Hermit retreats to some cave, that is to say, if he has the luxury to do so, all he'll ever question is this: 'What is my need, really? Can I even name one?' This latter question, however, presupposes a lot of discarding to begin with, for it's difficult to shed the capitalist schooling that will have you convinced that your life is all about giving in to fears and desires. When the Hermit shows up, you can be sure that he's ready to tackle head on this very marketing strategy that relies on inducing fear and desire in anyone who is unable to ask the simple question: 'Fear of what exactly,' or 'desire of what exactly'? When the Moon is also in the picture, we'll be in for a real rejection of nonsense. We can all rejoice. The Hermit is our savior, actually. He is not about existential issues, as your classical literature on the Tarot will instruct you, but about saying, 'I don't think so. Whatever bullshit you have for me, I don't need it. You can threaten me all you want, but I'm telling you, I need nothing at all.' If there's any wisdom in the Hermit's position, then it's in his utter rejection of cultural pre-conditioning and habitual patterns.

THE WHEEL OF FORTUNE

In questions about *power,* the Wheel of Fortune suggests you have none. You have power by virtue of existing, but in the larger scheme of things, considering also all that connects us, there's no 'I'm special.' You are not any more special than the others who are also caught in the wheel. Things go up and down, and you go up and down with them. It's not sure you get to know who's pulling the lever. One thing is clear: it's not you who gets to decide.

If the Wheel of Fortune is next to Force, you get the idea of what happens when you resist the course of things far beyond your control. You can try to overpower the situation, but it's not sure you can succeed. If you do succeed, it's not sure that you'll be proclaimed a hero and given a medal. The best you can do is look at the others who share your predicament and show some compassion. Competing is useless. You can be bold and hope that fortune will favor you, but that's playing a game of chance. Playing games with your luck can be very entertaining, but it does not mean that such an attitude confers power onto you.

You may not exactly associate the Wheel of Fortune with lack of agency, but this is where you're at when this card is in the picture. The only wisdom here is to know that things change. The question of who is to be master belongs to a different category.

FORCE

In questions of *dominance,* Force suggests that the premise for your actions is strong. The conditions for you to win are in your favor. All you need to do is raise your voice, or get your hands into the hair of the beast. You do this reluctantly, you lose. The beast will overpower you. Why would you be reluctant? Well, think about it. There's such a thing as 'political correctness,' 'me too' manifestoes, and other such cultural revolutions that make you reluctant. While you deliberate to what extent you can allow yourself to overpower the beast, the table gets turned on you. While you investigate to what extent you're on the same page as others, you lose momentum. Not good. Sometimes recognizing the fact that you can't negotiate with the beast is the best way to go, political correctness or not. So what if others will think you're dominant? What if you must be just that, dominant? Letting an animal's howl be the voice of the advocate is not always a good idea. Transmit coherently, but know also when the ones you're talking to speak another language, and act accordingly.

If Force is next to the Devil, you can be sure that what you'll get out of it is misunderstanding of the gross kind.

THE HANGED MAN

In questions about *'who done it,'* the Hanged Man suggests that it's best to let it go. You're hanged, and that's all you need to know. Unless you yourself are into acrobatics, someone else did the hanging. You may sit there and wonder why anyone would do such a thing to you, but that helps you little with your predicament.

I like to think of this card as describing a situation that can't be helped. If it can't be helped that others hang you, for whatever reason, you might as well take the inverse view, and practice the art of acceptance. One way or another 'this too shall pass,' as wise man Solomon used to say.

You may regret the fact that you're powerless, that others hate your guts and try to rob you of your agency. You may even regret what you've done that justly caused your hanging, but it won't change the situation. Swing like a pendulum with this mantra in your head: 'It can't be helped,' and then see what happens.

If the Lovers card is nearby, you may think of Cupid going for the rope that ties you, rather than any of the beating hearts. One arrow will be enough to split it. If you have enough power left in your body to realize your sudden release, you may even avoid breaking your neck on landing.

Otherwise, lord have mercy on your soul.

DEATH

In questions about what is *urgent and significant,* Death is your friend. Like a true Zen master, Death instructs you to start with a premise of negation: 'Not this, not that. Off with their heads.' The trouble with urgency is that it makes us mistake the essential with the inessential. This is very stressing. Death says, 'if you can't figure out the difference, it's best to say to yourself: I may be clueless about what's significant in my undertak-  ings, but I'm pretty sure that it's not this or that approach that I want to take.'

Sometimes it's easier to figure out your own truth, when you consider what you most definitely don't want to do, no matter how much pressure you may be under. Killing it starts with killing the illusion of actually knowing what's significant. It may be urgent that you don a new costume or identity, but make sure that before you do that, the crown fits your head.

I like it when Death reminds us that it's infinitely smarter and more rewarding when we stop doing what everyone else is doing. If you want to get a sense of what's really significant, you must swing the axe, chop some heads, and level the ground. Essentializing to the bones pays off more than saying, 'maybe this is also something I can do,' especially if any of the 'suit' cards are in the picture. 'Maybe I can also embody this Empress, if only I can make my declaration of intent loud enough.' But maybe you want to stop falling for hyperbolic speech. It's not even funny.

TEMPERANCE

In questions about *focus,* Temperance suggests that you must know what you're mixing first. How you mix your apples and oranges is the second question. But more importantly, Temperance invites you to ask yourself, as you stand there all tense: 'Why am I doing this?'

In all the Tarot literature I've read, I haven't seen anyone else ask this question when Temperance was in the picture: 'Why am I doing this?' But it occurs to me that this must be *the* question: 'What is the purpose of all this focus? Compromise, the smoothing out of tense relations, interesting alchemy, balancing the act, or regulating flow?' It would be interesting to witness a Tarot reading session when the reader goes straight for the question of why. Why all this perfect mixing? What does it serve?

If Temperance is next to Judgment, I can get a clear sense of how she prepares the bath for the naked people. But next to the Hanged Man, her purpose is not so clear.

Make sure you know why Temperance does what she does when in the company of any of the cards in the Tarot pack, as it's not sure at all that your answer would be one of the set phrases you've heard before.

THE DEVIL

In questions about *lies,* the Devil suggests that you look at the depth of a narrative and see how shallow it really is, unless you insist on finding yourself as one of the chained imps, actually enjoying your symptoms.

Think for a second about this spiritual discourse: The Buddha said, 'find the answers to anything and everything in yourself. There are no others you can go to.' Now consider what people do: They want depth, heaven and hell. They want to go to charismatic gurus whose promises know no margins. They want to be saved according to the good magic book: 'Yes master, please cross the threshold to the underworld for me, and speak with your most important guides, or better yet, make that the Devil himself as that is so much cooler. Yes, master, I understand that it's not easy to win the battles with the demons, but I'm sure you're competent, as you said, and after having crossed 7 seas and 7 mountains, you'll be able to speak to the first shaman in line who will disclose to you what my secret name is.'

I mean, really. Let us say no more, before the legions will get us. If the Pope is in the picture, the Devil asks you to ask him in the confessional to cut the crap on lineage and external 'help.' The only valid narrative is the one you create yourself.

THE TOWER

In questions about *perception,* the Tower suggests a reality check. We tend to think that what we build is stable and solid. We get behind doors and the view of the outside gets narrow. Even if you live in a modern house, where the windows can't get big enough, you'll still be missing quite a deal. Being outside doesn't help either with the wide perspective. You can know the things you surround yourself with, but seeing them every day doesn't contribute to the expansion of your point of view.

Being in a Tower is like being in a Tower. Enjoying the safety of its walls will only last for as long as the roof lasts. Any house requires maintenance. You can perform it regularly or leave it to chance. When external conditions hit, however, the most common response is to panic. Panicking is a terrible state, as it leads to total loss of nerve. In the spur of the moment you may think, 'that's it, I may as well take the jump into the void, and finish this,' but this 'thinking' is not thinking. It's anxiety, apprehension, consternation, hysteria, and dismay. The only cure for panicking is running a reality check. But how are you going to do that, when your response is not rational?

When the Tower is in the picture it asks you to consider the art of contradiction and paradox. Especially if the Tower is next to the Lovers, or the Fool. For the Lovers, there's no such thing as a reality check, as the winning perspective is postponed. The Fool has a way of acknowledging all differing opinions as being 'right.' The people to the left: 'The Sun is rising.' The Fool: 'Yes, you're right.' The people to the right: 'No, the Sun is setting.' The Fool: 'Yes, you're also right.' Meanwhile the Tower crashes.

In the midst of paradox there are many wondrous answers. Have you noticed that when you're hysterical you tend to laugh? Ask yourself why.

THE STAR

In questions about having your *wish* granted, the Star suggests that while it's a good idea to not believe in anything, it's a good idea to have faith, faith in your own naked being. When you put off your clothes to go to bed, how often do you think of the importance of how others see you? I bet it's zero times. No one is that stupid, to put off their clothes and still think that the most important thing in life is that others think well of you.

Generally it helps to adhere to whatever the current trend for beauty is. If you possess the kind of contemporary ideal for beauty, your luck is made, as beauty is still what makes the world go round, coming second to money. That one still wins. And yet. Let's go back to your nightly affairs. Here you are, naked, and presumably free of the anxiety induced by the cultural threat and demand: 'You must be beautiful, or else...'

When the Star is in the picture, it simply asks you to consider to what extent you can be magnanimous in the face of fake auras.

Consider the idea of aloneness here, because that's where the 'mystery' is, in this aloneness. The Star understands an old wisdom that most people don't these days, namely, the wisdom that says that whatever you do, you must do it without the wish to be validated. The Star makes offerings, but consider this: do you think the Star stops even for a second to check with her 'target group,' or the list of testimonials, because hey, people 'relate?' Speaking in terms of trends, there's nothing as enticing as being able to say, 'I can also be a star. I can see that it worked for this other person to drink the brilliant elixir and get this thin, so I'm going to do it too. I'm not alone in the world with my miserable self. Others are also miserable, I'm so glad, and lo and behold, here's the secret drink too. The answer to my ugliness.' Now, that's very reassuring, isn't it?

If the Star is next to the Magician, beware of the tricks that are being pulled on you, unless, of course, you love a fantasy tale, in which case, enjoy the magic carpet.

THE MOON

In questions about *influence,* the Moon suggests that you look at how impressionable you are. Social media is a great channel where you can test your spine. The more echo chambers proliferate, the more there's the illusion of strong conviction. Expert self-appointments abound, and power structures are subtly instituted on the premise that if we can't all be a star, then we're most

definitely all magical. 'Woof' the dogs of the world say, even though no one really knows what they are talking about. But there's the pretense. Meanwhile, let's just say that dogs howling at the moon are still dogs howling at the moon. They can seem frightening, so there's the tendency to quickly follow, as you never know when they might bite your head off. Such madness, to follow someone because you're afraid of them...

When the Moon is in the picture, it asks you to ponder on what fills your mind, what preoccupies it. If the Moon is next to the Hanged Man, you can be sure that it's a sign that you give in to the influencing, pulling forces because you're intimidated.

If Force is in the picture, you may think of just what you have in common with the ones who don't really speak a human language. How can you be on the same page as the wild ones? Unless you're willing to shape-shift yourself, it may serve you to look into what's being projected and how that fits your reality.

THE SUN

In questions about *relationships,* the Sun suggests symmetry. If you make a step towards the other, and the other makes a step towards you, you can have a conversation that's informed by mutual respect. The good news in such a relationship is that you don't have to waste time convincing the other of what's valuable. If you know it, and the other also knows it, then you can have a meaningful transaction. No one is cheating,

and no one is bullshitting. There's no need for masks and costumes here. Nor is there a need for 'identity.' Everyone is almost naked, and free of having to put up a front or act in inconsiderate ways towards the gratification of self-interest.

The Sun next to he Devil, however, is bad news, as we're here with pride and a hidden agenda. There's also symmetry here, but it's all about serving a master you don't know, one that enslaves you by telling you that what he does is good for you. You believe it because you want to be like the master. You will serve brilliantly, but not for a good cause.

The Sun makes you prone to seeing things clearly when the conditions are auspicious, but on occasion, the garden you find yourself in is not exactly Eden.

JUDGMENT

In questions about *experience*, the card of public space, Judgment, suggests that you die for yourself first, and only then participate in the public discourse about what it's been like to be dead. Why am I thinking of this? Consider this exchange as it's very common, one I've come across recently. Reader of Tarot books in a public forum: 'I've read this book and it's trash.' Response: 'Another one bites the dust. Thank you so much for this. You've just saved me dollars and time.' My silent response to the one in a hurry to bow out of having a personal experience of the 'trash': 'Aren't you so clever?'

I used to invest time in looking at the profiles of the people who make statements based on endorsements, especially because I've noticed an odd phenomenon. As soon as the gratitude is performed, the person who declines 'the trash' is then more than willing to appear authoritative on the content of the said trash, often in another social media setting. I don't want to say that it remains a mystery why anyone would claim to know anything about a product that they never engage with, as such is the function of the social media, to enable all sort of voices, but I am interested in where this type of false broadcasting gets us.

When Judgment is in the picture it asks you to pay attention to who you follow, or who people at large follow. Is it a loud voice with zero experience, or an actual authority? Personally, if I take an interest in a new trend that's trumpeted ever so loudly, I make it a point to invest both time and money to experience the thing for myself. Sometimes I win, and sometimes I lose. From the point of view of experience, however, I win every time.

If Judgment is next to Death, I'd develop a practice of running. Running away from fools who think that they know everything, who live by proxy, who have no lives at all, no experience, and no authority. To say that such people are as dead as a coffin would be an insult to the coffin. So much for the idea of enlightenment and awakening that Judgment presents us with.

If you want to participate in the public discourse where knowledge is shared, make sure you actually know what you're talking about first, or you exercise the art of distinction when you listen to others. Not all who yell and point fingers actually have the faintest notion of what it means to be a critical thinker.

THE WORLD

In questions about *impact,* the World suggests self-reliance. The mainstream Tarot literature sees this card as a sign of accomplishment and security.

Fair enough. Then we hear about the 4 evangelists protecting the world. That's also fair. But if you paid close attention, you'd realize that this card tells you to mind your business. The allies may be there backing you up, but you don't have to depend on them. In fact, quite the contrary.

If the World is next to the Hermit, you may want to take a closer look at your friends. Why would you trust them? Because they say that you can? What access do your allies really have to your inner world? The natural wreath that surrounds you is not one of their making.

When it comes down to it, only you alone know exactly what it took to get those laurels. You're sovereign when you're self reliant, not codependent. Orchestrating the world from that position of confidence and excellence is not only something to aim for, but something to practice when you remember what you are, and what your place in the world is exactly.

There's a reason why the World is complete. Nothing gets in and nothing gets out. All things are settled here. There are no more questions left to ask.

THE FOOL

In questions about *deceit,* the Fool suggests that you start with looking at yourself. What do you fool yourself with? I like to ask this question on April Fool's day. This year my reflection on that day was based on the observation that, at the collective level, we tend to fool ourselves about our significance.

Here's a string of questions for contemplation that you may want to consider: to what extent do you think of whatever you do as being awfully important? Why is pouring your soul into whatever you do awfully important? Are you sure you're not fooling yourself in thinking that what you do is awfully important? What would happen if you stopped thinking that what you do is awfully important?

The Tarot literature sees the Fool as a symbol of freedom. I prefer to look at the cards from the point of view of assessing their cultural function. The Fool bumbles about without an aim and direction. If he's free, he pays a price for it, often in the form of others pointing a finger: 'What an idiot.' Being an idiot, and hence unreliable, is not a desirable state, but being in a state in which you don't value your existence according to your sense of self-importance is bliss. When the Fool is in the picture, it asks you to think about your disruptive force. How often do you disrupt your habitual patterns? If it never happens, then I suggest you start asking yourself the questions that probe your entitlement to feel special, significant, and able to make a difference.

Try being an idiot sometimes. You will gain more than the intangible idea of freedom. You will gain peace of mind.

If the World completes the circle, the Fool opens it up. You're free to ask questions. A good starting point is this question: What am I?

THE CATCH

The point of going through the cards as we've done here is to give you an idea as to just how unsettling we can be with the cards, while at the same time staying very close to common concerns. A precise reading of the cards always operates with a catch: You can see things clearly, only if you see beyond the names we give things. How do you do that? By constantly maintaining a questioning mind-set.

As much of the occult world is invested in transmitted traditions, whether we're talking about a lineage or personal gnosis, I'd say that the only way in which you can make sure you stay away from clichés, flat discourse, and unverifiable claims is if you question everything.

As far as I'm concerned, reading cards is about seeing what is not, that is to say, seeing beyond sets of rules and conventions. While acknowledging the symbolic order of things from which there's little escape, the diviner can train herself to simply ask: Why do I think the way I think? What informs this thinking? How heavily loaded are my mythologies, and why should I believe them? Cards are mirrors of what you make of them, not of what transpires in heaven or in privileged access to a supposed secret.

WHAT TO ASK THE FORTUNETELLER

Since we're with the question, let us also have a closer look at what is a good idea to ask a fortuneteller about. Imagine this cry:

'My boss is an idiot and we can't work together, help...' This is a classic situation for a fortuneteller who is called upon to impart her impartial wisdom about the blind spots at stake.

But the inverse of the situation can also occur: 'Help, my boss is an excellently competent person and there's mutual recognition of what we do. And yet we clash. There's some resistance that I can't comprehend. What do I do?'

I look at two cards: Temperance and the Star. You'd think that these are good cards calling me to recite as if from a dream what the good books dictate, pointing also to a future resolution that's comforting. 'Temperance means balance and harmony.' 'The Star means inspiration and goodwill.'

Stubbornly I apply the mantra that I share with my students when it comes to recitations: 'This means that. No, it doesn't.'

It's all about what you see, not about what you know. And this is what I see: Not on the same page. One is holding water. The other one spills it. So the problem is one of incompatibility. The perceived lack of communication, in spite of excellent competence, leads to lack of cooperation. In the end, each of these ladies is wasting her time.

I'm enemies with what wastes my time. It's my biggest challenge threatening my claim to being Zen. If only... But I'm working on it. What the conscious mind has a hard time perceiving, I allow the visual images of the cards to inform me about. There's nothing like busting a blind spot, a preconceived or projected idea. An excellent boss with whom you're incompatible is not good news. It leads to nothing but trouble. That's the message. So we're not here with predicting the restoration of balance à la Temperance and the Star, without motivating why exactly we think so. The other hearing this message can do her part. She can go home and reflect on what causes incompatibility and then act accordingly. She can come back to pose more questions. What can it be?

Let's have a look at what I think is a good idea to consider. Classical questions can be divided into areas of concern with love, money, health, and work. But they can also follow more specific themes.

'Does he love me?' can turn into a question about resentment, dependability, or about how to cope with a parasitical, unrealistic thought about what's expected.

Questions about work can also follow the more specific theme of how to create and experience a symmetrical relationship, as in the situation when you extend yourself to making two steps towards fulfilling your duties over and above what's stipulated in your contract, and then, ideally, you also want to see that your boss makes two steps towards acknowledging your particular effort that goes into it.

Health questions can follow the theme of causality. What if it's not a physical condition that causes you to bleed? What if it's stress? And if that's the case, what particular area in your life has become so resisting to knowing it, resisting your conscious mind, that you can't even put your finger on it? As a general rule, what you don't know, you can't control, so it's a problem.

Questions about money can easily follow the theme of mobility, migration, and transition. A good question to pose in this direction is one that helps you realize that it's not here that you'll make more money but somewhere else. Where is this place, and what must you do to get there? More money is not always about how to ingratiate yourself so you get a raise, but rather about how to eradicate your fear of changing lanes or geographical landscapes.

Questions can also be of predictive nature, or of a more metaphysical nature. You can go from: 'What will I have for breakfast tomorrow?' to pondering on 'what's the meaning of life?' while you're eating cornflakes, a choice that you've just divined for.

Questions can have a descriptive character. Asking a 'what' question will give you insight that describes a situation: 'What's the situation here?'

Questions can be analytical. Asking a 'how' question will give you insight into the necessary steps you can take towards solving a problem: 'How will I cope with no income in the next month?' can disclose very concretely what is a good idea to perform.

Questions can be of reflective nature. Asking a 'why' question will give you access to depth and understanding: 'Why did he leave me?' can send you reflecting on what went wrong, making you comprehend why you're feeling the way you do.

Generally, you can also ask questions that combine the field of emotion with a practical level. You can use deduction to connect the dots or to create a connection to others.

You can use a question to transmit knowledge about a situation that you're unsure of, that is to say, by formulating a coherent question you participate invariably in making clear what's unconscious or vague in your head.

You can use questions to strengthen your trust in others, or to strengthen your faith in your own clear judgment, perhaps even about the value of self-reliance, in which case trust in others is eradicated or deemed redundant.

Mostly questions have a coping or a strategic character, as in, 'how do I do this concretely?' but it can pay off to pose some questions that have an investigative nature into the underlying premise and structure of what 'this' is exactly to begin with.

'How do I put up with my imbecile boss?' is a question that presupposes clear knowledge and insight into another person's motivations, actions, and psychological mind-set. Are you sure that when you deem the boss to be an imbecile that is also the case? And what if the boss's imbecility is directly a manifestation of the way in which you are or act on the job?

Asking questions is easy. Asking the right questions is hard. Then there are the questions that arise from the encounter with the fortuneteller, with the beauty of her words, inspiration, and sincerity.

'Why aren't you promising me anything?' you'd want to know, but you'll find yourself settled in truth with her answer: 'Because there's no tomorrow.'

WHEN JUSTICE IS YOUR FULL STOP

THROUGHOUT THE YEARS of reading cards, I've developed a practice: No matter what cards I read, or how many are on my table, in my mind I add Justice to the string. I want Justice to act as a full stop, and as a statement of clarity: 'It is so, beyond any doubt.' That is to say, the statement 'it is so,' only appears after I'm done rejecting what is not the case. If I feel that I'm close to falling into the trap of 'this means that,' what I quickly do is activate a mantra: 'No, it doesn't.' I try to keep my conceptual thought in check all the time, paying attention to how what I've learnt – for instance, how 'Justice means truth' – actually fits what is the

case. The reason why I call on Justice, so to speak, has to do with the fact that if I don't know what the truth of a situation is, then at least I can aim to be crystal clear about knowing what is definitely *not* the case. And what is definitely never a valid case, is the following, all at odds with the idea of truth and justice: Sweeping generalities, entitlements, intangible abstracts, and ungrounded proclamations and opinions.

If there's something that Justice abhors above all, then it's opinions. Opinions are entertaining, but if you want more from your cards than gossipy notions that don't go anywhere, or idealism that stretches to the end of the world, then you must think of ways to concretize and formalize everything you say about a situation.

To give an example: if you have an analytical bent, that is to say, an inclination towards reflection and investigation, then you will find it very hard to follow the discourse that has grand concepts such as 'healing,' or 'how to be successful' in focus.

What is healing? What does it mean to say that we all have wounds that need healing? How do we know that? And if this were to be the case, that we all walked around with stories of victimization and powerlessness, why is focusing on past trauma beneficial to anything?

What does it mean to say that there's a 'lesson' in everything? What lesson? What is the purpose of categorizing and labeling our experiences as 'lessons?' Is it because such labels will make us feel better about life? One would think that figuring out what's significant is more important than serving ourselves narratives that make us feel better about ourselves. Where is Justice in all of this?

Let's make a general statement that's valid: life has its ebbs and flows. There's nothing special about having a bad hair day, nor is there anything special about being on top of the world. Neither lasts. Devising strategies of healing your hair, or maintaining your success is a complete waste of time. There are more important things to do, such as have fun, play a game, smell a flower, or swim in the ocean. These are activities that are within anyone's reach.

What Justice does in the Tarot pack is thus ask such nasty questions about our tendencies to go with what most people do. People do what others do, old wisdom has it, and that's fair enough where living life according to dictations is concerned. But if you want more, then you must find your own justice.

How do you do that? You can begin with taking a simple step. Imagine Justice talking to you, remonstrating you: 'is somebody on the internet talking about healing or success again? Turn that shit off, close your browser, shut down your YouTube channel, close the self-help book. You're wasting your time. Look at what *is* and formalize that.'

Sit in silence. Don't think: 'I'll sit in silence for 5 minutes, 20 or 30 seconds because I don't have the time for more.' Just sit in silence. Ask yourself: 'what is my Justice?'

Here's my example in three cards.

I read the Pope, the Tower, and the Devil like this: my Justice is to preach towards bringing down establishments and all their enslaving lies. My justice is to po(i)ntificate about attachments.

A tough act to follow.

How about you? Maybe Justice will be part of your string. If that is the case, then imagine it also at the end of your string, putting a just full stop to your contemplation. If Justice is not part of your string, find it in the pack, and place it along with the other cards. Let it seal your sentence. At the end of the day, it might even address a question you don't ask, one about your reason for doing this, read cards.

JUSTIFYING YOUR JUSTICE

People often ask me: 'why do you read cards?' The answer is straightforward: 'I read cards because cards simplify relations, and through the simplification of relations I receive clarity beyond what I think is the case.'

In truth no one knows anything about anything. Therefore the sages of old say, relax; relax about having to do this or that, heal your soul, get empowered, follow a 12-step program, fix your shadow and your alchemy. These are all very entertaining acts, but they are not acts that give you insight. Healing yourself, and because of that supposedly empowering yourself, has a history of lasting about five minutes. Then what? I'm always interested in this 'then what?'

Healing yourself and working towards success gives you an opportunity to desire more, to experience more. But experience generates more experience, not insight. Real insight is beyond any clinging to acts of healing or becoming successful through any kind of personal experience.

As an aside here, I've dedicated this book to Nisargadatta Maharaj – let's call him a lucid man and my 'chief guru,' if I believed in that. He had a way of pounding on my 'experience' until I got what he was talking about. Experience is a word, as Justice is a word. Beyond the word, there's nothing that I should waste my time on. Damn. Just when I thought...

As a community of linguistically endowed people, we assign meanings to words. But do these meanings have fixity? No, they don't. They are not even fixed in the language that produces them, let alone fixed in something outside of language, if we can even imagine such a place.

Some ask me in disbelief: 'if we discarded the idea of healing and self-healing, then what's left?' Now that is a good question. What's left is freedom. If you're free of any duties and obligations that are in vogue, free of having to heal yourself, or having to be successful, having to make an impact on the world, having to make a difference, having to conquer the world, or having to score the bank, then you're left with insight.

Justice is the one who asks you: 'are you sure you're who you think you are? What are you? Who are you beyond a name? What is your point of reference, point of origin? Is it in the belly of a mother that you now hate, or in the spirit of an ancestor that you now fancy?'

It's not for me to say what I like or dislike about the world, or the spiritual world in particular where identity, self-empowerment, healing, and success are the major keywords everyone goes to. But I will say this: none of these concepts are useful. Not even by a long shot. What's useful is to answer the question of what you are, beyond resorting to yet another label.

If you're in doubt about your cards on the table, imagine Justice at the end of your string, staring at you, calling on you to recognize what your own justice is, calling on you to cut off your attachments, and to hold your acts of chopping wood and carrying water in check. After all, when you live and breathe as you do right now, there's nothing to heal, nothing to be successful about, nothing to boast about. There's just gratitude for knowing the difference between what creates schism, and what crosses the deep waters.

When Justice is part of a string of cards, it asks you to pay particular attention to your truth as a diviner. How much method and how much intuition goes into your reading? As far as I'm concerned, intuition and action spring from the same source and share the same momentum. When intuition equals clarity, your offering of truth equals flow, that is to say, your own justice has the capacity to re-create lost connections – the presupposition here is that when people come to you for clarity they do so because they feel disconnected and not in flow.

Your cards read the invisible acts, that is to say, while you read the cards to identify how you go from A to B, the cards themselves give you a hint of the space between A and B. What's happening there, in the space that's not articulated by any cognitive or emotional field?

BURN HER

Imagine this scenario, and how you would respond to this question from a person who has problems at work with an envious colleague:

'How can I burn her?'

You can test yourself. If your first impulse is to put the cards on the table and deliver a message such as it is, then we can say that your intuition and action spring from the same source, namely, reading the cards for another without judgment and beyond attachment.

If your impulse is to ask follow-up questions, exhibiting bewilderment too, then we can say that your own motivation is not so clear, displaying hesitance that reveals a contaminated mind. If you went 'what do you mean by burning her?' you would be taking a moral stance already. You would be tempted to correct the person's ways and say, 'you simply cannot do that.' You may even dismiss the person altogether on the grounds that now you've seen it all. You may tell yourself some version of a story about what's ethical and what's not, thus legitimizing your 'non-reading.'

In light of what the aim in cartomancy is, here's a question for you to consider, one that takes your own justice on board: how useful is your hesitance and judgmental position?

The aim in cartomancy is to make clear cuts. If you thought about this, you'd realize that even though you may have a different position on what the aim in cartomancy is – such as helping others with their problems, helping people realize that they're asking the wrong question, make correct predictions, consult on strategies of love and war, empower and enchant – essentially what you want is to make a clear cut, to deliver a sharp answer whose precision is so transparent that even the most opaque of minds can see it.

For your method part, the part that Justice stands for, look at the cards and understand for yourself what is at stake when you think 'function over symbol,' timing and momentum, and rulership and connectivity as they play out in context.

For clarity, consider your every word. How loaded is it, as in, what belief underlies it? How widely circulated, and therefore clichéd, and how straight?

The question: 'How can I burn her?' can be answered thus by these three cards on the table: Justice, the Tower, the Devil.

'First you assess methodically where her vulnerable spot is. If it's the head, then drop your bomb on it. Don't let her know it was you. The Devil is not into taking credit. Keep it underground.'

Now think: if this answer horrifies you, you may want to consider why. Is it because in other 'ethical' circles the diviner would show a 'better' preference? 'You can make her understand her own envy and help her get rid of her demons.' But think again: While this answer is non-conflictual, is it a precise answer?

For all intents and purposes it is not. It is not precise for the simple reason that it doesn't answer the question. It assumes a position of reconciliation, where none was asked for. It also implies a set moral action, where none was asked for.

The better answer would be to help the other figure out what her own bomb is, and why hitting the house, rather than something else, would do the job.

Clarity is not subject to judgment. Justice can tell you why.

WHEN THE CHARIOTEER IS OUT OF HERE

LET'S STAY WITH THE TOPIC of self-help, now that we're at it. In terms of my example with the cards, this one also features the card in focus in the wings, as the Charioteer was not part of the first three cards down, but showed up as the fourth additional information carrier.

But first let's deconstruct the card, unsettling it from its symbolic associations with victory, before we see how it works in context. Most standard meanings of this Tarot card will tell you that the Charioteer is all about coming: coming victoriously, coming home to be celebrated by the town, coming into character. This is true until we realize that, in actuality, there's also a going: going away or getting away very fast.

In all my cartomancy teachings, I insist very much on making this point: all readings are occasioned by a context and its question, not by lists of 'traditional meanings.' Logically speaking, it follows that your interpretations are, in actuality, also occasioned.

As a consequence, your response to the cards must be occasioned by what you see happening right now in the cards, not by what a fortuneteller said in the past that has now become a whole institution that issues directives and regulates symbols. Lists of meanings *can* be derived from commonsensical associations, but unless they are occasioned by your reading, you might as well ditch them.

I always say, use lists wisely, not indiscriminately. Don't just go, 'Victory!' when you see the Charioteer. What if your reading is occasioned by a situation of cowardice, or by a situation of good fortune, when you grab the opportunity to say to yourself: 'I'm so out of here?'

Not long ago I had an occasion to speak about the difference between doing contemplative work – in the style of Zen deconstruction of language – and self-help, which I see as exactly the opposite of deconstructing grand narratives, or what we also normally know as 'naturalized narratives,' such as, for instance, the idea that men are better drivers, there's heaven and hell, women are the first sinners, and children lend you respectability.

In self-help the Self is in focus and Help is also in focus. This presupposes that the Self has inherent existence and that Help is something the Self can benefit from, the presupposition also being that the Self has free will.

In Zen parlance the Self is a narrative, a fiction based on interpretation, a set of beliefs that, contrary to what is maintained, doesn't move mountains, doesn't win confidence wars, and doesn't enlighten.

Let's try this again: there is a self and the self can help itself.
Really?

I ask you this: 'can you hear all that? What do you think that all these words are? A representation of reality?'

Think again.

Self-help providers know all about the fiction that goes into the narratives of self-interpretation, or else they wouldn't be moving so easily along the axis of shifting stories of self-empowerment. Where it goes wrong, or becomes downright dishonest, is when there's insistence that there's an authentic core, an inner spark and authenticity that you can uncover through various methods, all leading you to your true self.

In the context of my conversation about self-help, these cards came up: the Fool, the World, and the Wheel of Fortune. The fourth addition, the Charioteer, was a card added to the three in response to my desire to see what else the Wheel of Fortune was doing, apart from going up and down. The subtle lever on the image invites us to look at the horizontal axis too, and ask: Who's pulling the strings? The Charioteer.

I simply said the following: the Fool comes to the promised land. The promised land turns out to be more of 'the same old same.' As the initial question was one about action and how to deal with a particular pagan community, the presence of the Charioteer here was not so clear in what it was suggesting. What's the appropriate action? To stay or to go?

The immediate observation to make here is that if you base your reading on the standard Tarot vocabulary, you'd never even think about questioning to what extent the Charioteer is coming or going. Nor would you think of the implication of it. The answer would be clear: you're victorious here. This community is safe.

But now think: what will occasion your reading of the Charioteer as a story of success, one of coming victoriously and celebrating, especially when, upon closer inspection, what we're dealing with is actually a world of disappointment?

If we pay attention to the image, how does the Wheel of Fortune *feel,* coming after the World? Is the World keeping its promise of elevation and oneness? What happens to the people? They all look dehumanized, caught in a place devoid of individual power and agency.

The Fool being a fool, all excitement and no distinction, thinks that he arrives at the right place, but do we get the same sense when we look closer at these cards and the way in which the progression is going? We go from one fool to more fools.

As far as I'm concerned, the Charioteer says this: 'I came, I saw, I conquered... my foolish belief that the lauded world actually has something of value of offer. How stupid can I be to hop on that wagon? I'm out of here.'

I said to my sitter, 'it's not a good world. Get out of it.'

Next time you see your cards, just think about what you're saying, and how occasioned what you're saying is by what is the case, not by what you 'know' to be a fact simply because others said so.

WHEN THE WHEEL OF FORTUNE IS NOT ABOUT PLANS

'WHERE DO YOU SEE YOURSELF in five years?' How about this answer: 'In five years I'll be exactly where I'll be, in the same NOW I'm in right now.' I don't know about you, but I find this question about positioning your future self in some desired fantasy identity as one of the stupidest questions I can think of. It's even worse if it comes from people invested in the spiritual arts, especially the divinatory arts, such as cartomancy, astrology, and oracle readings. Let me make this clear: no matter how much you want to stretch it or tweak it, the divinatory arts are not about new management. The divinatory arts are not about establishing relevance either, especially *your* relevance. The divinatory arts point to your positioning in the very moment you happen to pose a question.

The most famed oracle among oracles, the oracle at Delphi, while passing judgment in prophecy and prediction, always pointed to a current state. When the Pythia said to Oedipus Rex, 'you will kill your father and marry your mother,'

what she pointed to was very much the profane state of things that Oedipus found himself in at the moment of posing his question. The greater, obvious 'reading' that she gave Oedipus was to say to him: 'You are here now.' Did he understand that? He didn't. As soon as he was done, he ran horrified and thought that if he just removed himself from home, from NOW, he would avoid the crimes. He paid a hefty price for acting according to being in some imaginary future. At the same time, this amusement ride on the Wheel of Fortune got him, as it gets us, exactly there where we're always at.

We're always there where we're at. This happens as a matter of life happening as it happens. It may well be that, in hindsight, we can conclude that a self-prophesy has come to pass: 'five years ago I said that I was going to be the curator of a museum, and here I am curating away,' but if this happens it will not be the result of your acting on your imagination. It will be the result of external conditions favoring your acting.

We're all caught in the Wheel of Fortune. We think we have agency and can get off the daily routine and habitual patterns. We think we can transform and become something other or more than we were yesterday. We think we have influence and impact. We think that we make our own luck.

There's no such thing. We're always there where we're at. Nothing more, nothing less. Hence it's a fallacy to think that when the wheel of change turns, it places us right in the middle of our five-year plan. The sages of old knew this, and therefore insisted that our only duty, if there's a duty, is to simply relax and pay attention to where we're at right now.

What's the purpose of adding to the regular life pressures the one of self-expectation? Identity games à la 'how to manage your life so that it's more productive and successful' are the least interesting. What's more interesting is observing how what you know about yourself enters into play with observing what you know about the positions that are available to you right now.

When we talk about having the power to act, we don't talk about where we see yourselves five years from now. We talk about our sense of momentum. How strong is it, how clear is it?

EMBODIED ATTITUDES

I once gave a talk about embodied attitudes that are visible in the public sphere. I referred to mine as being resolute, ambitious, industrious, and indomitable. 'Oh, wow,' somebody said, and then remarked with a sigh: 'I wish I could be as precise about my own attitudes, as that would give me clarity in my decisions about the future and what to embody in terms of desired identity.'

I laughed, and I said: 'it's Saturn in Aries in the 11th house ruled by Mars in Virgo in opposition to Mercury too. That's what gives me this string of words.'

'Huh?' the person said, and then I laughed some more. 'Huh?' was the appropriate response.

The thing is that we can all come up with a string of words that characterizes what we're all about, if we took the pains to observe ourselves for just five minutes.

Where do your thoughts bring you? To an imagined future aligned with the clever questions that management theories in vogue dictate are interesting? I strongly doubt it. If anything, your thoughts will take you to the past. They will take you to the time when, as a 12-year old, you were an avid reader of a particular kind of books. Mine were all about swordsmen, fencing, warfare, martial arts, and tactics. What do I do now as a 50-year old? The same. I maintain the same spirit of fascination with brilliant war strategists, diligent and skillful masters. I still read books about chivalry and Zen samurai, and I hardly ever watch a movie that's not a Japanese or Chinese historical drama.

Where will I be five years from now? In five years the world will be as the world will be, with me in it or not, exactly according to what the future NOW will dictate. I will be in the NOW, as I'm in the NOW now.

Will being in the NOW be the result of my efforts? Not by a long shot. Knowing your NOW in the NOW is not mere word sophistry. It's your destiny. While we're all equipped to know this without special training, most of us prefer postponing the insight because of the allure of a desired identity: 'Tomorrow I'll be queen.'

THE WHEELING PATH

I read the cards for the astonished person who wanted to know about his path. Three cards fell on the table: the Lovers, the Wheel of Fortune, and the World.

I said: 'whichever road you take, it gets you exactly where it gets you. You will know what that is when you'll see it, because you'll be right in the middle of it, recognizing it – that is to say, if you cared to give yourself five minutes to observe it.'

I made an additional note as to the fascination with astrology. I said this: 'if you want to hear that story, you don't need a 50-page report. All you need is a sharp analyst who can relate the planet with the most power to act in your chart to the stuff you read when you were 12.'

What did you read when you were 12? What was your fascination with? Try to answer this question for yourself, if you want to concretize your NOW in a more nuanced way. Forget about imagining where you'll be five years from now. Don't waste your creative power searching for what is right under your nose.

AN ESOTERIC TURN

The esoteric meaning of the card of the Wheel of Fortune is construed around the idea of 'fortune, success, elevation, luck, and felicity.' These are the keywords that influential occultist A.E. Waite gave in his book, *The Pictorial Key to the Tarot* (1910). What I'm interested in is this question: how do we go from a wheel – spinning quite concretely even though seemingly counter-clockwise, if you look at the movement of the creatures in it – to such abstract notions as felicity? It gets crazier.

Even Waite, who was notoriously invested in symbolic systems of correspondences, felt he had to say something, or do something about the 'not so obvious' notions broadcast in his time. In his own book he laments the fact that prior to his understanding of the Wheel of Fortune, the associations have been much more aberrant, pointing to Eliphas Levi's time when this card was conceptualized as having to do with 'mean principle, fecundity, virile honor, ruling authority.'

Now, as this is not a book in Tarot history, but rather in seeing what there's to see when we look at the images of the Tarot for the purpose of expanding our field of vision beyond habitual ways of seeing, I don't want to make a fuss about other people's efforts, critiquing their stretched or lax ideas. My point is that it pays off to consider just how useful grand notions are when all we want to do is be here, not with some imaginary 5-year plan that may or may not be under the influence of 'virile honor' or 'felicity.'

Granted, the ones seeking the oracle want to hear about the very thing, the aberrant and the abstract, but if we know better, would we do them service if we complied with their wish for what is safe? The obvious is never safe, hence the wish for the myth... The subtler message in our card reading here has to do with recognizing the consequence of being impressionable, and listening to women who fight for your attention, the result being a disconnect connector. First a round in the amusement park, getting dizzy and not seeing the others you share the wheel with, and then all by yourself. The wreath in the World card is suggestive of a better wheel, so here the prediction can be said to take the tone of auspicious progression. But the fact still remains that, however you want to put it, you will be right there where you will be in five years, or five minutes from now.

In their sophistication the cards instruct us in this very Zen insight, quite far removed from the field of French and British occultism. The World is the NOW. The Wheel may turn, but the NOW stays. That's the only plan there is.

WHEN FORCE IS ON THE DOT

MANY SEE THE CARD OF FORCE in the Tarot as a representation of strength. In invented stories about this card, the woman with the lion is an archetype of power; not social power, as we reserve that for the Emperor, but power that has to do with character and moral spine.

Fair enough.

But if we are to look at the card from the position of having firsthand experience of it, rather than from the position of succumbing to other people's stories about it, then we can see that this card has a very peculiar function, namely, to instruct on how to deal with what is inferior to one's own standing. Although we acknowledge this as the most immediate response we can have to this card, in most narratives about it, interestingly enough, we find an insistence on other 'lessons.'

You will hear people talk about this card in terms of a lesson in strategies of overcoming resistance, or as a lesson in diplomacy of cautionary nature that we find in the old wisdom: 'don't bite the hand that feeds you.' Even more contrived is the lesson in getting in touch with your animal passion and magnetism. There's no end to what the 'little white book' can come up with. Again, fair enough.

But what interests me here is what is closer to what we can term is a correct response to the card; 'correct' not in the sense of there being a superior 'meaning' to it all, but in the sense of what is there prior to thinking and over-thinking. That is to say, what exactly can we see when there's nothing there to see, when we deliberately leave out of the equation 'what we know,' concepts such as power, passion, and possibility? What can we see when we don't universalize?

In the context of diplomacy, what if the hand that feeds you belongs to an unscrupulous person, dealing you hidden and not so hidden double and triple agendas? Are you going to rise against it and bite it, or are you going to bear it?

In the context of overcoming resistance, what is the appropriate action? To let the inferior who never gets it just be, or force your superior values down his throat? To what extent do you engage in making preliminary assessments of the situation, before you decide what the correct response is in relation to it? Your function as a reader of cards is to make such identifications that pertain to discriminating between what the cards suggest is the situation, what the cards point to in terms of positioning, and what the cards address at the level of function.

The card of Force in context and action can tell you something about the quality of resistance, how you position yourself vis-à-vis this resistance, and how you see yourself making the ultimate discrimination between what is superior and what is inferior in your own attitude, or that of the 'thing,' the 'creature' or the 'beast' that you think you need to 'passionately' overcome.

How annoying are you? Mostly I think of the card of Force as testing the level of our annoyance. We get annoyed, or we annoy our sitters with just about anything that suggests serious change or a head-on confrontation with our illusions and fantasies.

We don't seriously want to engage with the inferior, 'animal' side of a simple and primitive, yet strong and superior question. We don't want to answer the question of why we eat, why we have children, or why we need an identity, because we intuitively know already that if we were to give an answer 'before thinking,' then we would lose the social comfort that anchors our consciousness in dictations: 'I eat so that I participate in the communality of the act; I have children so that I can mirror my narcissism in them – when they exhibit signs of being successful, that is; there's another story tagged to the inverse of the situation; I need an identity so I can *be* somebody, sell something, have things, or have the power to influence others.'

The card of Force tells you to confront what you know by listening first to the lion's roar, yelling at you: 'how do you know this?', 'are you sure this is so?'

If you read for others, be prepared to annoy them. As a general rule, people don't come to the diviner because they have mastered the art of acceptance, the only art that gives you peace of mind. People come to you for your strength, a force that they hope will mirror their predicament, and fix it. And you *can* fix it, because you have clarity where they don't. Yet strength is not about dominant power, but rather about identifying how you respond to each connecting dot in a situation, so that you end up functioning precisely on the dot, and not outside of what is called for.

People won't like you much for seeing things as they are and leaving it at that – 'it rains' – while adamantly refusing to sympathize with their lamentations: 'I know it just rains. But it pisses me off.' Seeing things as they are is never about what comes after the full stop – 'But it pisses me off' – for what has liking or disliking to do with clarity?

'I hope you can help me overcome my loss. I lost my lover on account of doing a stupid thing. Do you think you can help me?' someone wanted to know.

'I can help you,' I said. 'Let me see what the cards say. Here come the Lovers, the Sun, and Force.'

'Three become two. Are you with this man now?'
'No, I'm not.'
'Then accept the fact that he's with someone else.'
'But that's the problem, that I can't. You gotta help me.'
'I *am* helping you. Stare at the two, not the three, waiting also for Cupid to readjust the point, and then say to yourself: *I'm not in this picture.* Get that mantra down your throat and you'll be set.'

AS A MATTER OF FACT

Being on the dot means being beyond forcing. The reason why you can fix everything ever so smoothly is because you know what language is and what words are. As words do not designate reality, only a representation of what we imagine reality is, we're in a perpetual state of magical enchantment. In order to know that this is so, all you need to do is look at the motives for why you bought your latest item. Even if it's food that you justify with your need for survival, ask yourself why it's the Kellogg brand of cornflakes you went for, and not something else. So you're subject to how people use words, for better or worse.

Sophisticated diviners have always been interested in how language works, with some proclaiming that they only 'tell it like it is.' It's a noble aim, if only there wouldn't be the thing called metrics, the thing called, 'what I see is subject to interpretation.' This means that if there's any truth to the statement, 'I tell it like it is,' then it's in the fact that it's forced. Is telling it like it is telling the truth? What would constitute the truth? Intuition, method of seeing things, words of sympathy and empowerment, ethics, divine inspiration, lineage, or something entirely other?

I have particular clients who are only interested in the so-called 'matter of fact.' They pose questions of this kind: 'yes?, no?, how much?, how little?, and when?' – I read a lot for stockbrokers who gamble on the stockmarket.

Usually my answer to this type of question reflects exactly the nature of the question. I say, 'yes, no, this much, this little, and, how about April?'

Some would call this approach 'classical fortunetelling,' being 'no nonsense,' or being 'matter of fact.'

I call it interpretation. Even the thing that we call 'direct experience' – which is something that interests spiritually inclined folks – is subject to interpretation. The reason for this has to do with language and the fact that we have to name what we think, feel, sense, taste, touch, and see. As soon as naming occurs, bias occurs.

So what is it that we do, when we don't want to believe that, as a matter of fact, as per the old oracle: 'you will kill your father and fuck your mother' – the oracle at Delphi being famously matter of fact?

I like to relax about any tension induced by what I believe I'm doing when reading the cards, or think that I ought to believe, or that I must believe. I look at the cards and try not to kid myself about not interpreting, not seeing according to cultural constrictions, even when I may well train my eyes to see what's not seen ordinarily; now that I think of it, the fancy 'language of the birds,' the signifier for divination, is also a linguistic construct.

Perhaps I'm saying all this because I happen to have my morning coffee while staring Nisargadatta into his eyes – he sits in a prominent place reminding me of how, as a matter of fact, there isn't the meter that can measure the longitude and latitude of our bullshit.

With my gaze still locked in position, I imagine Nisargadatta getting his hands in my hair, and splitting the hell out of it. Will I complain about it, or bear it stoically, knowing that how I feel about it is just words, words, and more words?

WHEN THE WORLD IS NOT A CHEAT SHEET

IMAGINE THE WOMAN in the World card, perfect as she is, making demands: 'why don't you love me?' Or, 'tell me what you think of me.' Imagine the woman in the World seeing everything that surrounds her as 'validation tools.'

What I see that's common in the interpretation of this card is that the World is suggestive of a state we arrive at after progress, practice, a 12-step program, shadow integration, or some other similar '1, 2, 3, here's the ultimate key to your happiness.' Such an interpretation carries with it an implicit entitlement: 'I'm here now because I made an effort. Pay me respect.' But is this the World's reality? No, it's not. Somehow I fail to see how the woman here, not touching the ground, is all about the idea that 'the method,' 'the practice,' 'the strategy,' 'the self-love' – all happily trademarked – got her to her elevation. The World card is not about 'being proud of it,' being proud of the process. It's about self-reliance in that deeply mysterious sense of singular consciousness. What has belief got to do with it?

When we think seriously about the implication of how we habitually internalize and then rehash interpretations without thinking about their premise, what we do is deconstruct belief.

There are many in the world who would swear that what they call 'MY thing' really helps people move from A to B. That may be so, and it's all good. But is a method only about end stations, about moving in a specific direction with the sole purpose of arriving at a goal? Is a method about process and the geographical relocation of the soul?

Think again. What you see in the World card is a reality that's not dependent on cause and effect. There's no causality here: 'because I did all this, I got to this point. Hallelujah.' Programs and practices subject you to a point of view. They are not the thing itself. 'The thing itself' has an elusive nature, and thank god for it, because it's only due to this elusiveness that we get to move beyond principles, beyond rules and conventions.

SPELL IT OUT, AND THEN MOVE BEYOND IT

In my academic career I was a method theorist. In my cartomantic practice, it's about the same thing: I come up with a method that facilitates our understanding of complex matter. I theorize and philosophize about how we use cards, why, and about what's the most useful to internalize at the basic level so that we end up delivering a sharp answer to a question. But if method was all I did, I may as well join hands with the army of institutionalized spirituality leaders who devise cheat-sheets for how you cope with life.

The point I'm trying to make here is that what we do in our work with the cards is more than survive or help others survive.

The pack of 78 cards is not a fancy cheat sheet, with the World card giving you access to the master shortcut. In divination we do more than disciplining our fingers on how to hit the right keys on the keyboards of our lives. We don't push the archetype buttons, as if the 'larger than life' idea is not already part of us. We don't empower ourselves by pointing to the mythical aspect of our lives, as if it were separate from what we experience on a daily basis.

If the boss is an idiot, isn't he already a lion-dragon you try to tame? If your lover is clinging to you, making a fuss when you try to talk to another, isn't she the siren you want to hide from? When you encounter an obstacle and come to a fork in the road, isn't the old sage you meet a master able to help you, and if he can't, how about a pact with the Devil? He'll give you a tour of the underworld from where you won't even be able to escape unless someone else pulls you up again with the power of their magical flute or trumpet.

THE FOOL'S JOURNEY, A NON-MYTH

If the Fool undergoes a journey that gets him the mythical World, he doesn't do it as a process that's external to his discovery, or by following a method, as in 'here's an archetype, why don't you embody it so you can conquer the world?' Rather, when the Fool undergoes a journey that takes him to the World, he does it as part of the 'program' that's called 'life happens as it happens.' There's great intimacy in this natural unfolding of life, one that's disclosed in the World.

The World's power is in being intimate with itself. The World's power is not derived from pride, from memory, from looking back and saying, 'yep, I've donned the appropriate costume at the right time, and voilà, here I am.' That would be foolish.

I offered this thought to one of my students: true empowerment comes from the realization that we're always already intimate with the mythical aspect of our lives. The mythical *is* our life, not just an experience of it.

The World card asks you to look at what register you're subjecting yourself to. 'Costume,' 'goal,' 'practice,' and 'progress' all belong to the same register, aiming at transacting with and for your identity. How about you think outside of identity issues, identity reassignments, identity calibrations, or identity transformations? How about you think, 'what identity,' and 'why should I waste any time with it?'

Remember this: identity, the way it's commonly transacted with, is not 'you, the special thing,' but rather a set of manipulations with masks. If you're fine with playing with masks, then more power to you. As long as you know that you're not a set of rules, you're not an identity, a special case identity.

WHAT THEN?

Ask your cards: 'what am I beyond my goals and efforts?' For all it's worth it too, let's leave out the part of investigating into who or what defines your goals and efforts, as it's not even sure it's you who's in control. Just ask: 'what am I beyond my goals and efforts?' Be ready to witness the crumbling down of your most cherished beliefs, or pleasures.

Perhaps these cards, the Tower, Justice, and the World, will say, 'you're not your culture, your family or your tribe. You're your own justice. You are *you* above and beyond all the ideas that surround you, for better or worse.'

Use your cards too to ask about what divination is to you. As far as I'm concerned, divination is not about the experience of the future, love and relationship, work and strategy, dream and nostalgia, trauma and fixing it. Divination is experience itself risen in chance and by chance. It is clear insight fixed in the heart. It is a World that's self-sustaining, protected by totemic familiars and a fairy tale flower-house. But ultimately, divination is all its own.

It may serve you as well to think of the World card as being not about the end station, about how well things have been accomplished. Rather, the World suggests that you're beyond the level of storytelling. The World says, 'you're done with stories and myths.'

Stories are just stories, not reality. Reality is simpler than a story. Whereas a story requires all sorts of styles and conceits, reality is all about the void, or about what others have identified as the impermanence of all things. You recognize that in impermanence you're beyond the story level, understanding also what the levitation in the World card is all about. There's no ground to walk on, because there's no ground to begin with. A society is called 'society' because it's all about laying the ground for rules and conventions. The card of the World makes you think of the implications of being above structure.

In contrast to reality, stories are often constructed with an embedded promise for permanence. If you're a Christian, there's the promise of enjoying everlasting life in heaven. If you say your vows properly in church, there's the promise of everlasting happiness. If you're Pagan, you might stake your life on it to meet the Devil at the crossroads, pursuing the promise of unending knowledge. If only you could get thinner, there's the promise of everlasting beauty and success. All these promises are predicated on storytelling that operates with the manipulation of belief.

The irony of the 4 evangelists, depicted in each corner of the World card in the form of animal and bird insignia, should not be lost on us. Are we with belief here, or is belief something we leave out of it? This magic circle is ruled by selflessness, not belief.

WHEN THE HERMIT IS EROS

LET ME MAKE THIS CLAIM that's valid for me in all situations: nothing, and I mean nothing, is sexier than mental stability.

Several cards in the Tarot pack suggest balance: Justice and Temperance are the prime candidates, but when you think of it, even the Charioteer needs to be in control of his horses, if he's to get anywhere. The Star suggests peace of mind, the Sun stresses a clear agenda in the head, and the World spells out perfect awareness.

All good, but before you get there, to discerning what is just, or to mixing perfect concoctions, whether of the mind's fabrications or something else, what do you do?

There's one instruction only in the Buddhist canon of teachings that I find the most useful among the arsenal of spiritual schools and manifestations: 'take hold of your mind.'

Indeed, without taking hold of your mind, you won't even realize this truth, namely, that every phenomenon that arises in the mind is the product of the mind. Without this realization you go through life mirroring and identifying with reflections that have no substance, but that you think are fixed relations, stable, and worthy of your idealism. You praise your emotional intensity, and call your general dissatisfaction with life or dramatic roller coaster 'passion.' But what we call emotion is a phenomenon that arises in the mind, hence the product of the mind. You can't even think, or say: 'I'm emotional today,' without using words. And what are words? Symbolic glyphs that a community decides 'mean' something. Right. So now we know where we're at.

When the Hermit is in the picture, he points to the context where it's possible to distinguish between stable and unstable states of mind. What enables discerning between passion and drama, peace of mind and obsession, is the act of disengaging from the workings of desire through language.

What the Hermit does, when he retreats his steps from the conceptual frames of culture that dictate what he supposedly needs, is take hold of his mind.

Taking hold of your mind is the most exciting enterprise in my book, as I identify in this move a strong desire to just live life, ride the wave, and not give a fuck in a most detached way. I bring in detachment here, as the condition for not giving a fuck is understanding what projection is all about. This includes not only realizing that our minds operate with thoughts that are the product of language and culture, but also realizing that we can get attached even to our excitement about holding this realization of how the mind works.

Any form of excitement is the opposite of mental balance. Some would say, 'how boring, what makes us human and interesting is our passions, getting excited about the Devil who enslaves us so we can feel life throbbing in our efforts to exert our agency, enjoy the illusion of giving and receiving commands, asking Hekate and Hermes to respond to our devotions, and generally looking for fixtures that are as far removed from the idea of taking hold of our minds as possible.'

Indeed, if we must polarize the relations, I'd say that the card in the Tarot that emphasizes the opposite of mental stability is not the Fool but the Devil, as the Devil's business is to convince us that the altars we cling to are *it,* when they are not. Whereas the Devil's biggest business is to make us believe in things, the Hermit says, 'no thanks.'

In contrast also to the esoteric notion that, when the Devil is not just about our base desires and passions, he's Eros incarnate, I find the Hermit a more accurate expression of Eros, simply because he makes the realization that everything that's external to the mind is not life itself, but projected 'objects' that appear to the mind. I see Cupid stretching his arrow. I'm getting excited here...

In our encounter with the mind, we can experience orgasmic bliss that has a counter intuitive force to the one that has us fall into another's embrace: 'fuck all this,' the Hermit says, while knowing the void that both gives rise to desire and returns desire to itself. When the Hermit holds up his lamp, what he does is invite us to consider what we question and what we mirror.

As a quick experiment on how mirroring works, ask yourself about the nature of your statement every time you feel inclined to say, 'me too,' in response to what other people offer in terms of story. Where does 'me too' come from? Shared experience, familiarity, or the stylization of acts? On my part, I have to say that I'm suspicious every time someone says, 'I relate to this,' in reference to someone else's personal experience.

When you ask questions about the nature of what you're saying and why, what you do is disengage from cultural pre-conditioning. The consequence of disengaging from language and its discontents is that it makes you realize that just as the mind is a mirror, reflecting anything you put in front of it, so are your stylized gestures.

You owe it to your body and your corporality to know anything at all. The body learns through repetition and imitation. You see people walk on two legs, you stand up yourself and take small steps. You repeat the process and before you know it, you win a marathon and get a gold medal for it.

Where it goes wrong is when such stylized, repeated acts are assigned meaning. Walking is *not* the result of having understood the meaning of walking. Walking is walking. If walking has meaning, it's because someone somewhere created a narrative about it, a story, a myth that turned into a legend, or an instruction into self-help.

MIRROR, MIRROR ON THE WALL OF MY HEAD

We all live through mirroring, but not all of us identify with the reflections in the mirror. Some simply go, 'that's a reflection, not the thing itself' – secretly also relishing the idea that what we call 'the thing itself' is also language, and hence another reflection in the empty mirror of the mind.

Mirrors give us insight into what the Buddhists call 'relative reality'[1]. But the mirror itself is empty, which makes it a good

---

1   One of my favorite discussions of the terms 'absolute reality' and 'relative reality,' designating emptiness and the form of appearances respectively, is in the book *The Heart Attack Sutra* by Karl Brunnholzl (2012).

metaphor for the absolute reality, the reality that's beyond the conceptual, and as such immovable.

The Hermit's lamp excites our Eros, making us present to ourselves, following our nature that has nothing to do with the language of desire. Just as a stream of water runs down every time, following its nature and the law of gravity without ever asking itself, 'what is my purpose?' – so the one who takes hold of her mind follows her nature independently of the rhyming patterns that her mind is also capable of creating, rhymes between thoughts and their synchronous manifestation.

As I read the cards for many seekers of spiritual insight who are invested in knowing how to stay alert, I'm quite astonished to see how often the cards suggest that maintaining first a healthy state of mind via being present to the world of the senses is key.

The Hermit here, flanked by the Star and the Moon, seems to suggest the following: 'being present means noticing everything. If you do your thing, whatever it is, from serving nakedly to philosophizing in the dark, can you hear the dogs barking? If you can, you're present. If you're not aware of everything that goes around you, even as you concentrate on the one thing that preoccupies your mind, then you're not present. If you can hear the dogs barking, then the crazy becomes marvelous, an 'object' of fascination.'

Taking hold of your mind means getting naked to yourself, and dancing to the edge of town. The dogs are barking, the caravan is passing.

WHAT ARE YOU DOING?

In our investigations into how language relates to how we read images, stretching our imagination beyond what is symbolically agreed upon, beyond the set cliché and 'tradition,' I like what is suggested here in these cards, namely an ambiguity that I can't resolve. What's in the Hermit's gesture: is he looking at the Star, asking, 'what are you doing?' or is he saying, 'what are you thinking?'

I prefer to think it's the first, based on sheer curiosity, as the second question would disclose anxiety, as per the presence of the Moon at the Hermit's back, anxiety related to women stripping off their clothes, yet not showing any desire to be with the man in the picture. Culturally speaking, that's obviously 'wrong.' If the woman doesn't get naked for the man, then what is she after?

The Star wastes no words. The Hermit is excited by her silence. The dogs are still barking.

Who's to say what they're both are up to?

WHEN THE MOON IS NOT CREATIVE

I HAVE AS YET TO ENCOUNTER A DISCOURSE about the Moon card in the Tarot that will not start with 'creativity' as one of the Moon's primary 'meanings.' I have a problem with this, especially when, in dynamic reading consultations that are not informed by the 'little white book,' the Moon hardly ever points to a type of creativity that's also constrained, and hence useful.

The reason why we need constraints when we deal with the creative impulse is simply because without structure, there's no clear transmission. Think about artists and their need to explain what they do. The more abstract the work, the more elaborate the artist's statement. In other words, creativity that has no distinct form is without value. Without value, creativity is useless.

Value is entirely symbolic. Stories create value. Without a story, there's no 'sell.'

This means that if creativity takes place, then it's always at word level. The more sophisticated the words, the more powerfully loaded with pathos and promise, the better the story that sells. Understood in this sense, creativity has zero to do with shadows, partial light, impressions, or the unconscious.

So, let's see about the supposedly 'creative' Moon, if read like the Devil in the martial arts spirit of cartomancy that I've started out with here. But I'll do something different. Given its nature as a celestial body, the moon reflects the sun's light. It has no light of its own. Now, if we were to take the Moon as a marker of prompting a particular question, we'd have to consider the possibility that we would have a hard time coming up with one. We're in the dark here. Let's have a string of three cards on the table, and let that formulate the question for us.

The point of this exercise is to make us shift our habitual approach to reading the cards for a story, and instead try to read them for the question. I use this trick in a series of Tarot prompts in my teaching and work with private clients, when I let the cards 'pose a question' to me that I then share with the others. Let's see what I mean.

The example below was created for an private client who ordered a series of 11 such questions. I reproduce one of the prompts here in the exact form I delivered it.

At the descriptive level, the Devil, the Moon, and the Magician suggest the following: when you don't get it, it's difficult to take a course of action that's rational.

First there's the belief that there are no alternatives – that's always the Devil's job, to make you believe that there are no alternatives; it's not like when you're bound to addictive patterns or obsessions, you're also aware of it. If you're in the grips of the Devil, you need outside intervention if you're to get free. If the Moon's illusions are your rescue, then you're pretty screwed, as you just sink even deeper into the pool of not getting it.

Now the question: do you ever experience that? A sense of sinking into not getting it, with the result of frustration that turns into resentment? Such sinking into despair is in fact a good sign that there's something that keeps you down, so you can dig into it, check with your unconscious.

You won't be able to recognize what it is, as that's the job of the unconscious, to stay hidden from the manifest, rational expression, but you can start thinking about your mental resources. You can at least pretend to get out of the miserable situation and fake it until you make it. That's the job of the Magician. To get you out. But know that his solution is still based on a premise of faking it.

There's more: what are you in denial about? Ask your demons about it, and then let your mental capability imagine another world. Projection is good if you can direct it yourself, or orchestrate it. Projection is beneficial if you know that that's what you're doing, project for the purpose of gaining clarity for a new course of action. It is best to be aware of your projections, lest you want to lose yourself behind the face of the moon.

THE FEEDBACK

The reaction to my reading above was one of excitement, as the person who ordered the prompts shared with me her own take on the cards, before she read what I had to say – in fact, what makes the prompt series exciting is also this part, when you can test your own insight against the way I go about it.

Among the points she made about the three cards here was this conclusion: 'be creative with your solutions and make magic happen.' I said the following: 'I always have a hard time seeing where creativity comes from in the Moon card. In order for creativity to occur, it needs a level of consciousness and awareness as the basis for its expression that is entirely spontaneous, not informed by thought and emotion. In the Moon card there's no such thing.'

Traditionally, the Moon card has been associated with many things from which we can derive a notion of creativity. Chief among these associations are the associations with women, fertility and fecundity, cycles, ebb and flow, intuition, fear and madness. On my part, I get it that when women are pregnant and give birth, they participate in the creation of another human being. But why is that creative? What is creative about a natural process? What is creative about fear and madness, about cycles, or darkness? By its definition, the creative impulse operates with a constraining dimension, with craft and skill. Without constraint, rules and structures, the madman is just mad, not an artist, and the fearful person is just anxious, not a genius. A woman with a child is also just a mother, not an intuitive who has perfect clarity, the clarity that occurs before thought and is therefore unmovable.

THE POINT OF CONSTRAINT

Particularly in questions that call for being clear, on point, or indeed, call for strategies of being more creative, it's a good idea to think of what you call 'creativity' and what you make of the 'source of creativity.'

If the source of creativity is the unconscious that you, by definition, can never be conscious of other than through (in)auspicious stumbling into grace – for instance, when you have a dream that's explicit, or when you realize that your tongue just slipped and went ahead of your conscious communication, disclosing in the process what you really want or are all about – then you must consider how you frame what you want to say.

In questions of creativity without boundaries, what you need is not a self-congratulatory gesture that validates the vague, but rather a clear structure. Therefore, always beware of the Moon informing your plans and deliveries, whether verbal or visual. If you have to let others know about your deep idea, then think about how you structure what you want to convey beyond falling into the trap of seducing yourself with the fog in your head: 'Oh, the Moon card, I'm so creative…'

Muddled conversation has never seduced anyone, and it's not even sure that if we called the ambiguity in our head 'creative' or 'poetry' it will help much. There's only so much 'creativity' that people can handle. If the creative impulse is not consciously organized and orchestrated, then it's bound to remain in the realm of the merely insane. Some thrive on the insane, but as such, the insane remains a singular expression of no benefit to others.

We can be creative in our vivid descriptions of our passions, but the words must go somewhere, if they are to have value.

THE COLD MOON

In a recent reading about love, I was adamant in dissuading the person I read the cards for that the Moon, flanked by the Star and the Lovers, suggested a hot date.

Granted, the stars on the Star card are all suns really, which means that they possess enormous heat. But they are distant. The only star whose heat we can feel on our bodies is the one leading our solar system. All the other stars are too far away to make an impact. The Moon itself being devoid of heat is not a hot body. As for the Lovers, let's not even go there. What's so hot about ambivalence, about not knowing who to listen to, your mother or your girlfriend?

There may be a wish for the projected 'hot' love, but the reality of what stares us in the face at image level is quite different. If the Star is a creative lover, she'd have to come up with a strong strategy that would make the swaying man make up his mind. There's no indication here that she has that force. Alas...

WHEN THE LOVERS ARE RIDICULOUS

THE TROUBLE WITH THE LOVERS card is not only the fact that it emphasizes ambivalence, but that it also painfully demonstrates the consequences of being impressionable. Being impressionable has one effect only: to make you more impressionable.

In most of the Marseille type cards, our young man in the Lovers card is represented as such, living under the impression of how things are, not really being able to discern what is really the case.

I often get this card in the context of so-called toxic work environments, with the discussion revolving around the unfortunate situation when gossip prevails. Well, voilà, this *is* your gossip card, featuring an impressionable person who is not even capable of wondering who is right and who is wrong, let alone discerning between opinions.

Moreover, in this day and age of polarized echo-chambers, who needs distinction? The Lover at the center of the Lovers card can be said to be a representation of the people who don't even need to make any choices, as all it takes for the maintenance of being validated – a condition required by all the insecure – is to follow some big wolf in the group of preference. Questioning is not necessary, because the big bad wolf already knows everything, and you can just trust him.

Our impressionable young man can vacillate, however. You see him nodding to the woman on the left, hand on the crotch of the woman to the right. Presented with facts, he still hesitates. Presented with clear value, he still has to ask around. What if others disagree with these facts and values? Isn't agreeing or disagreeing with opinions more interesting than facts and values?

Welcome to the social media space. If you want to have an understanding of the Lovers card, pay attention to what happens on Facebook or Twitter. You declare that you've arrived at an understanding of something. Self-appointed masters will insist on disagreeing. The Lovers card types witnessing the conflict will go with the self-appointed masters without ever hesitating about this reality: what is the point *ever* of disagreeing with someone's understanding of something? How can you ever disagree with *how* someone understands a situation?

Imagine this scenario: I make a statement on Facebook: 'today, after much pain, I have finally arrived at understanding how 2+2 is 4.' The self-appointed masters will hurry to give me the thumb down and say, 'I disagree.' The impressionable ones will follow suit, for it is the case that when people decide they like someone or they dislike someone, what matters is not *why* that is so. What matters is following. One follows the important wolves *just because,* not because there's just cause for it.

'To be or not to be,' the Shakespearean lover, Hamlet, asks and then does something foolish that takes him out of this world. The world says, 'I disagree.'

So here's what I say: the Lovers card points to ridiculous situations, situations that are always perceived from a heavily polarized angle, when that doesn't have to be the case.

In connection with my Art Tarot workshop, my partner and co-director of Aradia Academy, Bent Sørensen, had a great insight when he presented some very blue, male lovers to the Aradia Academy Alumni group, featuring gay subjects. He asked a pertinent question too. I share his point here: 'consider the traditional meanings of the Lovers in the major Arcana: joyful union, if you're a sentimentalist; hard choice if you're a Marseille devotee. But what if it's not a binary, what if it doesn't involve any women – whether mother/daughter or rivals for your affection; what if it's all male and no choice is necessary?'

Indeed, it's a good question, and yet, when I think of the countless representations of the Lovers card, where we have three humans depicted on it, rather than a man, a woman, and an angel, as is the case in the Waite/Smith Tarot, then I can't help thinking that their demeanor reminds me of something. This 'something' is the posture that I find universal whenever I look at three people standing casually, disclosing exactly what they are doing, gossiping, fixing the world via exchanging trivial information, or flirting without any sign of serious commitment to anything.

BEYOND AGREEMENTS

With agreements and disagreements in mind, let's ask the Marseille cards this question – remember also that all the cards I get for these essays are based entirely on random draws, with the card discussed actually falling in that exact position.

What would happen if people simply dropped from their vocabulary this phrase: 'I agree,' or 'I disagree,' whenever they want to participate in a discussion whose premise is opinion and a choice of 'I like' or 'I dislike' that has already been made even before any verdict is out?

The Tower, the Wheel of Fortune, and the Lovers suggest the following: if people stopped agreeing or disagreeing with opinions, things would run their own course towards some action. Choices could be made on the strength of argument, not on the strength of emotion. Emotion may pull the Lover boy apart, engaging his hand, but he need not follow in that direction.

The Lovers card is not about following your heart, but rather about knowing your place, and acting from within in accordance with the positions available to you.

From a traditional perspective, the Lovers card has always been significant in divination, especially considering the idea of choice. As most people come to the diviner to get clarity on a difficult choice, seeing the Lovers card in play is always exciting.

But what is this card a marker of, beyond the general keyword, 'choice?' Only context decides.

A STUBBORN CUT

Think of this popular line flooding the internet, addressing the aspirants to success: 'what all successful people have in common is that they make decisions. They decide to decide.'

I want to fall for it every time, as some people can actually write in a very engaging and convincing way. But what does it mean to decide to decide? As yet, interestingly enough, no one advancing the claim that making decisions automatically places you in the successful category, has ever mentioned the trouble with being stubborn.

I come across many claims that are the result of people deciding to adopt a certain position, and often it's as clear as daylight that their decision is *not* the result of reasonable action or the result of exercising the art of distinction. People decide that happiness is a matter of decision. Fair enough. People decide to be devoted to a cause because it brings them satisfaction. Even more fair. But people also decide to love and hate for emotional reasons, a decision passed off as rationality.

The latter instance is interesting as it aims at moving the heart – one way or the other – and moving the heart is a mighty art. I'm interested myself in how I move the heart (mine and that of others), as it's within this act that we get to experience going through life in a movement that's not part of the illusion of having linear goals. I can see why the attraction to deciding to be happy is so popular, because it carries an implicit call to align your goals with those of cultural dictations. If you're not happy, you can't work. If you can't work someone stands to lose money, including yourself. If you can't make any money, you're a failure. Is this straight talk? It is. The only trouble with this straight talk is that it's false.

So think, if you ever feel the magnetism of the claim to decide to do something, be something, or demonstrate something, take a step back to investigate the tone and anchor of your decision. Is it informed by discernment or by stubbornness? If the latter, then be on guard, as stubbornness merely renders you closed off in your heart, experiencing the exact opposite of what it means to have a moved heart.

I can't even remember how many times the Lovers on my table pointed to this very problem with stubbornness, for it is a fact that when young people can't make up their minds, often because they lack proper knowledge, they get stubborn. Instead of admitting that they don't know, that they're not in the position to know any better and hence ask for some help, they invent all sorts that is detrimental to their standing, or what's even worse, they start listening to the crowd that's not invested in discernment. While everyone is having a good time gossiping, no one is the wiser.

A DISTINGUISHED WIDOW

As I grew up I had very strong lessons in the art of deciding from my mother. When my father died at 39, she found herself a woman at the height of her beauty and power. Many pressured her to make the decision to take another husband for her own sake, for her children's sake, for society's sake. Some were even so blunt as to directly point to her being a threat: You can't be a beautiful woman walking the earth unattached, and thus potentially lure the married men out there, who wouldn't mind having a go at the widow. One of my mother's most common answers to this was to say that she was not going to decide because making a decision feels good. She was not going to marry another man as a front for respectability. She was not going to decide that she will now be happy again. So she remained unmarried and stayed that way until the day she died. Many thought she was stubborn. But she was not. She showed distinction. Every suitor was carefully evaluated, and weighed. She made up her own mind about the men courting her, rather than letting herself be influenced by the opinion of others.

On occasion, I bring this stamina to the cartomantic table, the force that tells me to hold my position and not move an inch, but even after years of reading the cards, when I see the Lovers I feel the vulnerability of my inhaling breath. I actually hold my breath so that I won't give Cupid a chance to hit me with his arrow in my discerning gut, dislodging my heart.

Once someone asked: 'how can I move my lover's heart, so that he makes the right decision?'

I said the following, hiding a smile too when I saw the Fool, Judgment, and the Magician: 'You're a fool to think that you can move a heart to make the right decision. For the right decision, the heart must move on its own accord. You may think that making grand and loud proclamations will do it. But if the one you're aiming at is a magician type, then he'll want to know: what trick is this?'

While the Lovers card was not in the picture here, the card of Judgment mirrors it. Also here we find three people, with the angel as if deciding on their fate and fortune. While the desire to say, 'I'm saved by the bell,' may well be represented past the impressionable state, we're not with cards here that give us access to the moving of the heart.

The Fool knows nothing. The Magician knows a lot. In between them the public space. The honorable dead are rising.

When we say, 'to each their own,' we might as well say, 'to each their heart.' We are not connected in the heart with anyone else, contrary to popular romantic fantasies. The heart is a vast repository of wisdom and clarity. The Lovers don't have it. Lovers are cruel in their possessive passion. So they don't have a heart. They move with the ego protecting their interests.

If the Lovers card suggests 'decision,' what it highlights is competitive sport. To say that this card is about 'following your heart'[1] is an insult to the heart. We find love and the heart somewhere else than in impression or the race for winning over choices dictated by others. The Lovers here play a game of hands. Not all are lucky to grab a heart and know it. Some are at the mercy, chubby bum and all.

---

1 See among others, *The Way of Tarot* by Alejandro Jodorowsky (2009).

WHEN THE MAGICIAN DOESN'T IMPROVISE

AMONG THE ZEN MASTERS that I venerate, there are some who are not exactly either Zen monks or Zen masters, at least not by any of the definitions we impose on the people who are in the state of having clarity about everything.

Hijikata Tatsumi, the Japanese founder of the *butoh* dance, the 'dance of utter darkness,' usually sits right behind me at home, between an antique Tibetan Buddhist thangka from Lhasa and a calligraphy of the Heart Sutra. There's a reason for that.

I consider Hijikata profoundly Zen, in spite of his weird philosophy and performances. He is known for having said many strange things that, however, ring a bell with me. Everything he formulated in the form of principles around dance and life insists on choreography, as choreography gives you access to the most precise bodily movements that we have forgotten all about, partly due to growing up and subjecting to culture's ways.

Not many get 'the *butoh* thing,' as a *butoh* dance may look like something very haphazardly done, improvisation being in the high seat. But Hijikata himself hated improvisation, and insisted on choreographing a dance by using conceptual thinking and visualization that would be wrung through a naming machine, giving life to scenes and movements. For instance, if he decided that a dancer must dance 'a gold fish,' then the dancer had to follow 43 movements and 45 names of movements[1].

Since the 50s, *butoh* became more and more popular, but it's clear to anyone who is seriously interested in this that it wasn't because of Hijikata's stringency. I won't launch here into the history and controversies surrounding *butoh,* but there's something that I want to take from Hijikata to illustrate a cartomantic point.

In an interview he addressed why he opposed improvisation. He said: 'life is improvisation enough. I don't need it on stage too.' I find this statement utterly intriguing, because what it implies is an irony: everything that we improvise in life revolves around dictations. When we say that we need to cut corners, what we actually mean is that we need to devise strategies to bypass whatever cultural impasse we're at. When we improvise at work, we do so because of the unrealistic pressures on us. When we improvise in our relationships, we do it because we find ourselves subject to unreasonable expectations.

So indeed, who the hell needs fake improvisation in the arts, if we still grant it that the function of art is to move our hearts and to derail our habitual patterns of thinking, putting us back on track towards freedom? I'm with Hijikata on this one, because I can see how his insistence on not improvising is of great relevance to what we do when we think of the Magician in the Tarot, and try to read his 'improvisations.'

---

1 See *Costume en Face*, p. 133 (2015).

THE MAGICIAN'S ACT

Contrary to popular belief, the Magician is not merely 'good at improvisation.' If you think twice about it, you realize that improvisation is actually never on the Magician's table. Everything he does is carefully choreographed. He's probably right up there with what Hijikata would do: if he has to make a white rabbit appear, he would have a whole list of scenes and named movements that he would go to, that would enable him to not only manifest the white rabbit, but also go to the heart of it.

Whether in a traditional, cultural setting as a con man, or as a mediator between the above and the below in esoteric Tarot, the straight (or street) Magician is simply never about improvised acts. A fake Magician is. If the Magician is worth his salt, he is highly educated in all things staged and choreographed, down to the subtlest movements, facial expression, and costume. He also exhibits high discipline, perseverance, and genius, all in equal measure.

The Magicians who *do* improvise, what of them? I hope never to meet them face to face, though I come across them in all sorts of contexts. I see them getting high and mighty on their improvisational throne, all theatrical and no substance. Paradoxically, being truly theatrical actually takes a whole lot of work, not play, work that involves bearing humiliation from a master. Without humiliation, how are you to learn the art and craft of acceptance? The fake magician would never stoop to that, as it would mean exposing his limitations, and having to go back to the drawing board to polish on the failed act. Now *that* is too much work.

The Magician who improvises due to shallow thinking is thoroughly insecure. You know him by measuring the extent of his improvisation. The more improvised the act, the lesser the understanding of the premise for the act.

I've developed a habit of quickly noticing what I'm dealing with, whenever the Magician is in the picture: is this a Magician who seduces me with his discipline, and demonstrates to me how 'anything goes' is simply so *not* part of his routine for a reason? Or is this a fake Magician, conning the con, pretending to have worked on his act, when in reality he never?

I'm looking at Death, the Charioteer, and the Magician in order to get a sense of what makes a strong magician. The cards say, a magician who can eyeball the contrast between boldness and bones is a magician versed in study, that is, the study in how to pay proper attention. Polishing an act requires drive and an intimate knowledge of your costume. Cutting to the bones goes somewhere, often to the essence of the act, to noticing the obvious, a high art, indeed.

As a choreographer, the Magician is not a Fool, stumbling into things and taking pride in the improvised act, all in the name of some perceived idea of freedom anchored in a complete lack of precision. The Magician as choreographer tells a story by showing you his hands. Can you see what he is doing? Will you swear by the story of what you're seeing?

When the Magician is on your table, he invites you to ask yourself about what you prioritize in your divination: the cards, or the stories about the cards? I like stories, and I tell them myself with the cards, but in divination consultations I prefer the direct approach, which is to say the approach that prioritizes seeing the obvious, rather than seeing what others have told as a story.

There are methods that develop clarity and seeing the obvious without getting entangled in story and discourse. My strategy is to cut through the words and create with the cards a vast space in people's heads. I can only do this when I rely entirely on core principles, not on hearsay. Therefore I throw into all my teaching the rigor of Zen, because I like a clear head and sharp mental stability. Others prefer the emotional value of a story. The Magician knows how to manipulate with both in a masterful way.

KNOW THY MAGICIAN

Ask yourself these questions: How many times did you read the Magician as a Fool in a divination session, attributing to him the Fool's qualities, without realizing that what differentiates between these two cards is precisely discipline versus disorder?

How often do you consider the idea of stage, study, and choreography when you see the Magician land on your table, as against the Fool's improvisations?

How often do you think of the Magician's ability to show you the reason for his existence beyond the improvised act, beyond the colorful mask that bores you to death, because it's nothing but a cover for laziness and limitation?

I'm asking because it occurred to me that it's not very often that the serious magician stumbles into a rehearsed act, as a fool would. I think of the fools of the world who think they are magicians until you catch them with their pants down. The serious magician who is skillful is beyond reproach. That's precisely part of the act, the high magic. This type of a magician serves me to point out the consequences of dramatic sublimation, and what we tend to fall for when it comes to the discourse around the Tarot. Who do we listen to, and why?

My general intention in this book has simply been to let the deconstruction of sublimation be the nerve that runs throughout these 'portraits' that I try to depict. At the end of the day, I want my Magician to be Zen, and say to me: 'here's my act, perfected throughout many years. I've no idea what it means. I'm not here to improvise *meaning*. I'm here to choreograph the hell out of this dance of darkness, and eat you all up with my act, an act that comes in exactly 22 scenes and ten thousand names.'

SAME CARDS, DIFFERENT ANSWER

The cards here, Death, the Charioteer, and the Magician, also answered this question once: 'when can I retire and live comfortably?' I offered this idea: 'you can retire when the time is right, when the momentum that's called, 'up until here and no more' is on rolls. As to the comfortable, it's in your hands. Make it happen.'

Sometimes we must think of the Magician who does more than improvise, as someone who talks with his hands, casting a spell on himself. The Magician's hands are his words. That's the grand trick. Pay attention to the hands, and you'll be in possession of the Magician's secret, his language of the birds.

HIGHEST ACT

We could argue that the Magician's greatest sin is greed; greed for the attention of others, 'look at what I can do…' Greedy magicians are not so interesting. You can watch them for about five seconds, and then know that you've had enough already.

Conversely, when the Magician is not greedy, he has an important thing to say. 'Look at my table,' he says. 'Can you see all these things?' The audience nods excitedly, expecting to see how the many things on the table come to life in an unexpected way. But the real unexpected thing here is that the Magician will not use any of the stuff on the table for his act, especially when the stakes go higher. For this he will use you and your lack of attention. That's his weapon against the incredulous.

So the highest act that the skilful magician can pull is when he shows you that there's always too many things on the table that distract. If he discloses his trick, he will say that there's never more than one thing he operates. The things he shows you are nothing but props. 'Too many things' are not his thing. In this sense he is more minimalist than Death itself.

When excited women in love see the Magician on the table, I say to them: 'yes, this one is clever, but is he clever enough for the highest act?' 'Can you tell the difference?' they want to know. 'Yes, I can,' I tell them, and then show them the one thing.

WHEN DEATH IS A DEITY

WE HEARD IT BEFORE: Death is the great essentializer. It comes without warning, and it teaches the final lesson against all greed, the desire to live being one of them. But what if you thought of Death in the Tarot as being more than cutting to the bones, transforming life or endings? What if Death is the god of warriors and treasures, Bishamonten himself, or the Indian counter-part to the Japanese, Vaisravana? What if Death, not the Emperor or the Lovers, is a representation of strategizing well, which in martial arts parlance is the same as strategizing from the heart?

Once I had the pleasure of being interviewed four times in a month – a big deal for someone who prefers not to. Each time I was asked to say something about having cut my relationship with the academic world. Each time I offered the same simple reason: the academic world is a very sad and dull place, mainly because basic curiosity has become an embarrassment to academics.

You simply cannot tell academics that you research into the cultural manifestations of the occult because you're curious, without seeing them raise an eyebrow. Not only that, but you'll also see how the 'rational' academics are very suspicious of anything that smells of practicing the said arts. Never mind the professor of religion who goes to church every Sunday, practicing Christianity; that is allowed. Currently, many more academic researchers 'allow' themselves to be more visible about the occult that's on the rise, but they still don't do it because of curiosity. They do it because there's the pressure to study what's current. It's good that witches are now 'relevant.'

I made my cuts with the university because I find stupidity and hypocrisy unbecoming of the so-called higher learning institution. My greatest disappointment, however, has been to witness discrepancy in action: while you sit heavily on it at the top – you didn't earn your degrees and position for nothing – people take you lightly. They take you lightly because you insist on being curious about things and on moving with ease between the disciplines. You simply don't do that in the academic world.

When you're seriously curious, you find that you don't have time for greed, and if there's anything that you must not take out of the academic equation, then it's greed. You can't function at the top without being heavily invested in greed. You cut greed out, you're a fool.

Of course, the resistance to the people who are simply curious, and because of that devoid of personal interest, cuts deeper than the surface. A genuinely curious person will not have an ego construction and maintenance in focus. Quite the contrary. As soon as such investment occurs, if curiosity rules, then it also acts as an axe. This means that the curious is ready to kill herself, that is, kill all agendas of identification with any specific interest. This always comes across as dangerous to the ones living under pressure, the pressure to *be* somebody, embody a strong image.

DEATH TO BEING TAKEN LIGHTLY

It's always a nasty situation when others take you lightly, either by displaying ridicule out of defence, or by ignoring your already established authority. But there's something you can do about it. You can respond with a heavy dose of clarity, reminding everyone of how the great essentializer, Death, deals with greed. You can plaster Bishamonten all over your walls, and with good martial arts deathly resolve, you start strategizing from the heart. In this strategizing, you're beyond asking the question of 'why.' 'Why is there lack of recognition?' is thus not the interesting question. When Death swings its axe and heads are rolling, questioning others' motives for what they do is not essential anymore. When Death is a deity, it calls on you to know the value of your decision, resolution, and determination.

You look at your cards and say, Death and the Hermit mirror Alpha and Omega, the Magician and the World.

When people take you lightly, fling death at their greed, the greed they experience whenever they think they have a say in it where your place is concerned.

Imagine greeting everyone with these words: 'My place is beyond. My place is in my empty heart, now filled with justice, the stuff between magic and its realization.'

STOP CHOOSING

'Yes, but isn't there a way for reconciliation?' some ask about the situation of having lost the grip on their relationship. It's hard to see Death in the picture, followed by the Lovers and the Emperor. There's something unsettling there that the sitter doesn't quite know the implication of.

'It doesn't mean it's the end,' I say, 'but that you must stop choosing. If there's too much swaying, too much preference for one side or the other, you'll be stuck in confusion about what the appropriate action is. Make a decision to see what you see. The heads are down. What is there to keep deliberating on? Be resolute. There's no negotiation. Only the determination to stand your ground. Even headless yourself, stand your ground.'

In relationship questions, when Death appears it can suggest many things, but reconciliation is not one of them. In this sense Death is stronger than any deity we can invoke and haggle with. Death is beyond the relative plane where everything can be negotiated. Showing the anemic vulnerability of the Lovers, or the mental stretch of the Magician are not tricks that work here.

When the Emperor, or the general in the army goes to war, he's not thinking, 'let's see now, how can we all survive?' He is thinking about his own survival. There can be no negotiation there.

The three cards above speak of the impossibility to stay ambivalent, to think that you can still choose. If choice is in the picture, then it's for stepping up to making a decision. What comes, comes. As long as the Emperor has his eye on the ball, his own scepter and regalia, his attention is not distributed, not even to this lamentation: 'I lost the battle.'

What I like about the subtler message of Death mirroring the Emperor here is that it's about the usurpation of memory. What's the usefulness of thinking of the past, of haggling with memory? The Emperor turned his back to choosing, leaving the Lovers to their regret, or the question of who will inherit what.

When Death is in the picture, stop saying, 'yes, but.' Look ahead and rule.

WHEN THE EMPEROR LIGHTENS THE HEART

IF YOU SAW THESE THREE CARDS on your table, the Emperor, Death, and the Tower, you wouldn't think, 'a light heart.' If the heart would be in the picture at all, it would more likely be heavy.

Let me explain.

The Emperor's function is to rule imperially, issue edicts, strategize, conquer, and territorialize. He is the boss. We all know bosses, and they are all alike in performing the above functions. If there's a difference between bosses, then it's one of application: some bosses abuse their power, some are indifferent to it, and some underscore the essential in it.

With this in mind, let's look at these cards again.

What do we see? We see the Emperor in conversation with Death: 'first you take their heads, and then I'll go in there with my hammer and smash the house.'

Without a context for this reading, you're now welcome to speculate about the Emperor's motive for being so hard on everybody.

How about this idea? If the Emperor performs his function correctly, he is bound to be interested in dealing with people who receive his rulership with a light heart. Why is this important?

Imagine the opposite. You're a ruler who leads from the heart, but the ones you lead resist you; they are closed off to your vision, and as if that's not enough already, they also insist on not getting it. So what do you do? Negotiate? Scrutinize your own motives to make sure your heart is in the right place, or make a deal with death to take away the stubborn identity?

In many esoteric texts dealing with the description of the Tower, you'll find the association of the tower with identity and ego constructions. Indeed, identity doesn't exist other than as fiction in our heads, and the function of the ego is to make sure that we know our place. Not only that but the ego is also invested in protecting this place. It's an important job.

But when towers grow too narrow or too tall, the first thing that happens is that we lose our sense of situation and space. This is another way of saying that we experience our hearts as barred from seeing things as they are. With thick walls around our minds, acting according to our correct function is not possible.

With this in mind, think of the Emperor's ability to territorialize. How about letting him conquer your head?

It's easier to see the consequence of this if you have someone you truly worship, or someone who, once upon a time, has smashed your claims to crowns one by one to your great benefit and liberation.

For instance, there isn't a single day that passes when I don't read the words of the great master, Nisargadatta. I mentioned him before. I'm afraid of Nisargadatta. He sits on my dresser next to a bald Buddha, demanding black coffee and tobacco. I make offerings to him every day, and he responds with a question everyday: 'are you engrossed in concepts again? Fuck you.' Some would say Nisargadatta was a great spiritual guru, but to me he is a great Emperor who lightens my heart. I start my day with answering him back: 'I'm engrossed in concepts again, fuck me, amen.'

The thing about this approach, or indeed, dialogue with the master, is that there's nothing spiritual about it. Nisargadatta, who was adamant about the fact that we are *not* what we think we are,[1] would find no place for 'spirituality' anywhere in the equation that has our relative existence on a par with the absolute, with the absolute subsuming the relative. There's parity here because without the relative there's no awareness of the absolute. So it's a given that we are not what we *think* we are.

How do we know it? Show me a person who is not, at least once in their lives, suspicious of the premise for the condition of their existence. This is another way of saying that we are intuitively aware of the fact that all we ever do is wear masks according

---

1 Nisargadatta Maharaj's most popular book is *I Am That* (2012), but I find among many of his other works, *Prior to Consciousness* (1990), *Seeds of Consciousness* (1982), and *Beyond Freedom* (2008) stronger.

to how our linguistic competence enables us. What we are nobody knows.

When Death clears the path under the able guidance of the ones who know just what death is, what you experience is a lightness of being, space in the head, zero burdens and worries, and vastness.

When you territorialize your head, you lighten your heart. 'Tarotizing' with a hammer means getting rid of all belief.

You look at the cards and deliver what you see, not what you believe is the case: 'the Emperor means power. The Tower means the ego. The Empress means nurturing...'

When the heart is light, it has no trouble speaking in the voice of clarity: 'the Emperor and the Empress are having a falling out.'

Is there an implicit question here that we also hear? One that has to do with what to do about it? Let's look again. He smashes it. She holds her ground. You could tell these two to get back in the house and start yielding their power. Sometimes yielding is the only action that wins the battle and saves the bricks.

WHEN THE EMPRESS IS DISGRUNTLED

SOMETIMES IN CONSULTATION situations you get to have a sharp dialogue with the sitter, even before you lay down any cards. Here's a scenario: a lot of anger and frustration is put on your table before the visual language of the cards takes over. Successful woman in private business is not so successful anymore in her communication with her clients.

Woman: 'Everything was fine, and then all of a sudden, I feel all this resistance. I keep doing what I've always been doing, and I let people have access to a lot of free services, and it looks like now they're somewhere else in their expectations.'

Me: 'Do you have any idea what prompted the change?'

Woman: 'Hmm. Let me think. It all started around the time I invested energy in reading a ton on marketing, coaching, and social relations.'

Me: 'What is the gist of what you've learnt so far?'

Woman: 'That no matter what, I must always be grateful for the people who listen to me, as they might as well go somewhere else. At least that's what Seth Godin says.'

Me: 'True that. But let's think: what is presupposed in this gratitude? That when people listen to you they do you a favour and therefore you must bow to them? If you act according to this thinking, then you can be sure that this path will lead to the death of your business. On occasion, marketing specialists can be right, but if they assume too much, it's a problem.'

Woman: [Thinking about it] 'I see what you mean. So, what's the better approach?'

Me: 'Not to assume anything at all. You offer what you offer. If people listen to you, fine. If they don't, fine. They can go somewhere else. This notion that you have to be forever grateful to the ones who consume the value that you create is rather an expression of ultimate fear, leading to the death of your business.' I then further continued. 'Imagine this scenario: spiritual leader teaches about impermanence and the non-substantiality of all things. Students flock to the Zen temple, leading to the teaching becoming a successful business. Some time passes, and the students get tired of Zen philosophy and practice. Too much detachment and self-introspection. Off the students go to where they are allowed to cling to something. Something external, like Jesus or Solomonic magic, as all that other stuff about finding your own mind is too much work. What will the Zen master do? Change his philosophy to accommodate the students and thus 'protect' his business? Like hell. People come, people go. When they come, you say welcome. When they go, you say farewell.'

Woman: 'Oh.'

Me: 'Yeah, I guess Seth Godin would disagree, but then he's not into Zen. Let us allow ourselves to forgive him.'

Sometimes the fortuneteller engages in making such preliminary remarks. But what did the cards say?

Woman: 'Oh, wow, the Empress, Death, and Justice...'

Me: 'You got it. The Empress acting according to the rule of following opinions on the internet leads to her death. How about finding your own Justice instead? The idea that a business has to be like a family, where you get to nurture everyone, is an illusion. You are nobody's mother, and the ones working for your are not your children.'

JUST LAUGH AT IT

If we were still discussing the card of Death here, I would say that this example is a case of 'When Death makes you laugh.'

When that is said, situations such as the above are countless. Every week I get to read cards for at least three very angry and frustrated women. I've also been there myself, but fortunately for me, my peace of mind doesn't get knocked off so easily.

I often advise the disgruntled empresses to use their anger more ingeniously, by positioning themselves boldly against any assumptions. You're in business (private or public) for a reason. You do what you do without self-doubt, fear, or apology.

There will always be certain personages among your clients who will behave no better than certain personages on the internet, who object from the position of 'I know everything already,' or follow your work for the sake of debunking it.

Just think about it: if you say, 'I'm a financial consultant,' and the response is, 'yeah, but I object,' or, 'I'm a philosopher,' and the reaction is, 'yeah, you philosophize too much,' or, 'I'm a card reader,' and the attitude is, 'yeah, but your method is crap,' or 'I'm a woman,' and the conclusion is, 'I can see that, and I don't like it,' then what do you suppose we can call all this? I think 'stupid' would cover it. Turn it into a solid practice to discern between objections. The idea is not to be forever grateful to the ones who listen and then, when they stop, be angry and frustrated. People listen for a reason: only you can do certain things. The day they stop listening is not something you should worry about, and definitely not when you sit in your discerning power, following your own justice. What better success than that?

The cards here suggest that cutting the 'woman' out of the 'business woman' equation is a good idea, especially if the woman is defined in terms of nurturing, emotional response, and passivity. Business is business. What has it to do with pleasing others? If an offering is strong, it stands on its own. Anything else to 'support' it in the name of second-guessing others is a complete waste of time. Justice here in the final position simply asks: 'are you sure you can afford to waste your time? Is that the right thing to do? Adjust your posture and your method, not your fear. You don't need an unjustified show of gratitude.'

WHEN THE SUN NEEDS NO TRUST

AT LEAST THREE INFLUENTIAL BUDDHISTS and Zen masters are reported to have said that they never trust anyone. The three are D.T. Suzuki, Chögyam Trungpa, and Dainin Katagiri. A 15th c. manuscript at the Vatican also states that 'trust is the mother of all misfortune.' We're with the wise folks here. What's going on?

In their cultural constitution, our relational selves are based on trust, and it goes to show that without trust, there's no transaction. Our cultures and societies are built around our capability to give and receive trust. Those who fail are called traitors.

At a functional level, this is very simple and very clear: either you are reliable or you are not. But how clear is this reliability, when we want to talk about truth and its realization, which is something different than talking about relative and absolute states, or mundane and sacred manifestations?

That Zen masters don't trust anyone may come as a surprise to people living in a world where 'trust' is a highly valued commodity – you go to a Zen center or seek a spiritual master because you trust the teaching – but the truth is that in light of the impermanence of all

things, trust as a fixed, stable, and reliable entity becomes nothing but another subject to be suspicious of.

As with everything else, the question to ask is about what makes a situation trustworthy, what makes a relationship reliable, and what makes acting according to the situation appropriate. So it's not trust that comes first, but rather, responding to situations that have trust as a concept in a fluid and transactional mode.

If you think just a little bit about the obvious here, ask yourself: just how much point is there in trusting people, when people change all the time? What does it mean, also, to ask that others trust us? When we ask for trust, aren't we actually obligating others to rise to our expectation of reliability? We value consistency in the actions that follow the speech-acts, but when we do that, is it really trustworthiness as a stable thing that we value, or more the expectation that, 'if I do you the favour of trusting you, you do the same for me?' And when others don't rise to our expectations of consistent and robust behavior, then what?

Zen centers are populated with enthusiastic students who trust masters who don't trust them. Not all are aware of this, to begin with. Students are devoted in their love to the masters, while the masters keep a hard line that's called: 'I'm not impressed.' Some get the point of that, others take it personally. When the latter happens, it's easy to see how the initial trust turns into resentment that can quickly also anchor in stories of denigration, blame, and moral denouncement: 'another greedy Zen master implicated in a sex scandal,' as if a Zen master's sex life is ever anybody's business.

That last remark aside, as it requires a different context to unfold than the cartomantic one, what we can observe here that's interesting is the intentional asymmetry in the student/master relationship – which has a long history.[1]

Underlying this asymmetry is an inherent wisdom behind the scene of trustworthiness, where the master simply suggests that if you can act it, you can be it, be that devotion, love, reliability, trust. Whereas being enthusiastic is a mode that activates your emotional field, it's a whole other story when you act according to the situation – when you show diligence and simply just work towards better self-scrutiny.

Meanwhile, you simply don't say to others: 'I trust you' – though many do it on a daily basis without thinking. What I'm thinking myself is this: 'I trust you' is completely inappropriate, as it's devoid of correct functionality in relation to identifying properly the context of the other's situation.

When I say, 'I trust you,' what does 'I trust you' presuppose? That I know you, or that I know your situation? What do we actually know of others, even the most intimate ones? Nothing. Also, you don't go around asking people when you want to divulge secrets: 'can I trust you?' as this is an equally inappropriate way of putting it when dealing with sensitive information.

The reason why trust in such situations comes across as awkward is because it lacks illumination, which is what brings me to the card of the Sun in the Tarot. Graphically and at the level of the image, everyone can see that two people share their mutual trust. But how many think of the underlying structure to this symmetrical relationship: 'I give you my love, and you give me yours?' The Sun makes things clear, and it can also burn like a laser through muddled agendas. So here's what I think of the two

---

1 My favorite story here is the one about how the Tantric practitioner and Mahasiddha Tilopa (988-1069) 'abuses' the hell out of his disciple Naropa.

people in the Sun card: they invite us to inhabit the space where we can maintain double vision, that is to say, when we can maintain seeing the other from a double perspective.

The subtle question that we can ask ourselves here, as inspired by the idea of the double vision, is the following: how can I be flexible in my certainty about another? The inverse can also apply: how can I be flexible in my uncertainty about another? It serves us well to think that when gazing at the moon and minding our own business is not available to us, as far as having to act towards others is concerned, we can think of how to maintain double vision; after all, we have two eyes, suggesting that it's best not to gaze for too long in just one direction.

In the Sun card people see each other, which is why the Sun has traditionally been associated with vision, especially as it pertains to readings and consultations for health situations. But how flexible are the two children depicted here in this act of seeing, especially since seeing is culturally informed, often acquiring particular shades that's constitutive of identity? If we stay with this thinking, we may speculate on the reason why the designer of the deck and the woodcutter would represent children on the Sun card. Is it because they're not yet fully integrated in society?

WHY DOUBLE VISION?

One of my favorite literary critics, Gabriel Josipovici, has this to say in his brilliant book, *On Trust,* where he makes a very apt comment on what happens when, in our desire to experience the fullness of love, or its continuous expression, we forget to think of it in terms of its finitude once death occurs. He calls this situation 'the double vision' of the sense of life's abundance that entails the event of death, also as an abundance.

> [The] denial of the dual vision... in the end entails a denial of the world we live in and, ultimately, of ourselves as embodied beings existing within that world. Yet such is the nature of suspicion that, once unleashed, it appears to produce a totally convincing and self-consistent world, not simply an alternative way of looking at things but the only way there can possibly be.[2]

Zen masters are masters because of their suspicion and their ability to maintain double vision in doubting everything they know. When they say, 'I trust no one,' you can stake your life on it that what they're doing is demonstrate correct function in accordance with identifying properly what the situation always just is. If you doubt this, ask your cards: 'how can I love without trusting anyone?' Here's my example. Three cards fell on the table, followed by a fourth. They suggested the following:

---

2 *On Trust: Art and the Temptations of Suspicion* by Gabriel Josipovici (1999).

'You think you know what the other wants, and if you don't, you're willing to investigate. But think again, and then consider your commitments. What function do they have? 'Keep going' is the same as acknowledging movement, and that includes the movement of your consecrations. You can love without trust, if your moving is seemly.'

THE BRILLIANT AND THE DULL

Closer to a mundane consideration of the cards here, I have to say that whenever I come across this combination, the Sun followed by the Hermit, I always think, 'how can anyone try to illuminate with their small lamp what is already gloriously luminous?' So what I always presuppose about this situation is that the Hermit in question must be pretty opaque, or dull to not realize what stares him in the face.

On the question about loving without having to trust, what better cards than the Hermit and the Pope? While we may argue that the Pope is more invested in trusting the divine power that he represents, at the same time he's more a representative of the church, in charge of maintaining the rituals and the dogma. Neither requires trust, just performance. The Hermit trusts no one *par excellence,* so he's our Zen master here.

I chose to pick another card in addition to the first three to see what the Pope was blessing. I couldn't stop laughing when I saw the young man. In light of our discussion here of the Charioteer coming or going, I saw the Pope saying: 'just go, trust no one, including your horses. Life happens as it happens, under the sun shining brilliantly.'

WHEN THE POPESS GHOSTWRITES

I'VE ALWAYS BEEN FASCINATED with ghostwriters, and I've had the pleasure of reading the cards for a few of them. One of their common concerns is the following two-part lamentation: 'I'm writing for a schmuck, who has a name and an idea that gained commercial traction. I'm embarrassed to have *my* idea misrepresented.'

The first part in this statement refers to private and personal frustration. The second refers to misguided public representation. What bothers the disgruntled ghostwriters is that the 'writers' they write for are guilty of failing to make an important distinction between knowledge and wisdom. Nowhere is this more apparent than at public shows connected to the launch of a book. The gist of the ghostwriters' complaints can be summarized thus: The 'writer' is good at rehashing the principles that the ghostwriter has been good at formulating, thereby giving the impression of knowledge. But the thing about principles is that they are based on basic understanding. You can have quite a lot of knowledge, or be good at synthesis, but if you

don't also have understanding of *what* and *why* you know what you know, then you can be sure that this lack of wisdom is going to offend a few people who happen to know the difference.

For instance, one way in which I distinguish between books is by looking precisely at what the author actually understands regarding his or her topic. There's always something in the book that will disclose the level of understanding that's based either on reflection or on borrowed ideas. As for shallow thinking, I've developed a special radar that spots it immediately.

I made a whole career in publishing and making distinctions between knowledge and wisdom, and I can say with some degree of confidence that what moves the heart is wisdom, not knowledge in action as public show.

Apart from the books that fall into the category of what I'm trained to assess and what I've earned my degrees for – literature and culture – I like to read martial arts manuals. Textbooks in this genre are some of the best examples of how you can train your discernment, as it's easy to see who writes because the topic is popular and because googling information about it – that is then flung to the desiring public ever so fast – is accessible, and who writes because they actually have a basic understanding of what underlies the principles behind a style or a school.

Going back to the Popess, I see her as a representation of not only what it means to know secrets – the meaning often associated with her function in esoteric Tarot – but also what it takes to not divulge them.

When ghostwriters complain about their frustration, what they complain about is the secret that cannot be revealed regarding due authorship. They must honor their contract.

Many Marseille Tarot enthusiasts have noticed the fact that the Popess looks into the void. She holds her book in her hands in a gesture that's almost suggestive of dropping it, but her gaze contains a mysterious message. Perhaps what she's thinking is precisely this: 'you are not to divulge the identity of the Fool you're writing for.'

At least that's what I said to the woman I read the cards for, when I saw Judgment, the Popess, and the Fool on my table. She was tempted to go to the public and save her writing.

For a story about mainstream publishers that hire celebrity editors to make a hot name famous, I recommend Rebecca Miller's collection of short stories, *Personal Velocity* (2002). This volume is written with women in mind, and is initiated by the story of Greta, an editor also called the Grim Reaper, who does what there's to do to advance the author and herself – a better scenario than that of the ghostwriter who can only participate in advancing 'the author.'

Each of the seven stories features a woman who can be said to represent a version of the Popess who's challenged in her keeping or divulging a secret. In between keeping and divulging a secret I see this principle at work: action and temperament underlies the binary oppositions between writer and ghostwriter, woman and muse, wife and victim.

The point I'm trying to make here is that the way in which we read the cards follows our desire to go beyond the information and knowledge we can gain from the cards. Without processing the visual cues and information we receive, it's not very likely that we can gain understanding of any predicament, or of what we're generally dealing with.

Next time you see the Popess, don't just think, 'the Popess means silence,' as tradition prescribes. Rather, think 'words.' Think about the words that go into a narrative on all the levels that you perform on, as a reader of the cards, as a reader of books about cards, or as a teacher of cards. Ask yourself: 'is what you know the result of real understanding, or is it based on textbooks rehashing lists of principles and meanings devoid of wisdom?

When the Popess is the ghostwriter, she invites you to contemplate precisely on what sits between the secret and its revelation, between knowledge and wisdom, between claim and understanding. As readers of books, we often like to think about the author's motivations, about what they're like, what causes they fight for, and who inspires them. But why do we have this urge? How might it change our perspective of the words we read, if we knew that the author is *not* the author, but just a popular figurehead? The Popess asks us to judge a book by its content, not the cover, the gossip, or the flashy persona behind it.

HOW THE POPESS HERSELF READS

The Popess being a representative of the erudite knows what goes into the reading of both books and cards. Let's see what she has to say.

Every reading of cards is a three-part process: narrative, analysis, advice. Narrative is your act of creating a story based on what you see. The cards speak a visual language inviting you to humble yourself and see what you see, not what you invent as a 'system' – esoteric and mysterious or rational and analytical.

Analysis is what you make of it. It's more than interpretation, as it requires you to heed attention to the specificity of every individual context and situation, and then make a decision as to what the strongest argument is. The rules of logic are applied to what is possible and what is probable.

Advice is what you prescribe. Do this, do that, don't do this, don't do that. Advice is also a word of comfort, or a word that strengthens the heart. You get to the advice because you made an evaluation. After description and reflection comes the sentence: 'This is it. This isn't something else. This is it.'

Many come to diviners because their heart has turned to stone. They lost faith and trust. Because they cherish the concepts of 'faith' and 'trust,' if something is off, they get depressed. They can't say, 'this is it'. They feel that they need to test everything in order to gain clarity. But that takes time and effort. Most are not in acceptance of the fact that they lack the time to think about things, nor does it occur to people that 'thinking about it' is a cultivated skill. The realization that 'I don't have it,' the skill, that is, leads to frustration. Enter the Popess.

The first thing that the Popess points out is that resistance to acceptance leads to suspicion: 'what if I only function half of the time?' or 'what if I only get it half of the time?' And indeed, 'what if I can only provide ideas for half of my book, having to leave the rest to a ghostwriter?'

The Popess says: 'we're always subject to the 50/50 rule.' Once I said this to someone: 'I happen to have complete trust in the obvious, that what we live by is always a 50/50 thing, whether in love, luck, work, and money. This simple realization gives me complete peace of mind.'

I still stand by this conviction. What we operate with always, in spite of what most would have us believe, is variables of the 50/50. Sometimes we get it, and sometimes we don't. We are never beyond what's possible and what's probable. We can help things along by employing technologies of magic or science, but the fact still remains. The pendulum swings both ways: it's a 50/50 deal. When this got clear in my head, the first thing that happened to me as a diviner was that I stopped testing everything. There is nothing to test. There's just the poetry of living the magical life, which is another way of saying that you are able to appreciate what you do in the moment that you do it, taking also exactly one step at a time. The point is thus that living a life without projections is living a life beyond hopes and fears.

'THY CELTIC CROSS'

Let's look at 'hopes and fears' for a moment here, as it's a big concept in the Tarot world. It also ties in with the opening of this chapter, when I introduced the example with the frustrated ghostwriter.

In my own Popess activity as a teacher of cartomancy, I like to discuss classical texts and card layouts for the purpose of looking at their underlying structure. If the structure is weak, I take great pleasure in pointing to where it's weak, and because of that, I like to point to how it dismantles itself, even without my having to push it. The popular Celtic Cross is often a topic, and we investigate into the benefit, or, indeed, the disadvantage in having the cards locked in positions: 'this is you, this is the other, this crosses you, this is above you, this is below you...'

I won't go through the mechanics of reading this spread, as it's beyond my scope here, where I mainly read three cards. But I want to refer to an interesting dilemma. One of the students once expressed anxiety with having to read position number 9 in this 10-card spread as an expression of both fears *and* desires, referring also to many texts that are downright problematic in their take on how to read this position as a combination of two contradictory states.

In response to 'I don't get it, can you explain?' I pointed to language and said: 'I fear she doesn't love me' discloses an implicit desire: 'I desire that she loves me.' So, hopes and fears. It's that simple. Why people complicate everything for no good reason merely discloses their fear of being inadequate, which in itself carries the desire to be master.' The obvious strikes again.

In extrapolation, what the Popess knows is that our fears and desires are never more than narratives. We can analyze what's happening at this level, and even offer advice of this kind: memories and projections have no inherent nature. It's all semantics. It's all a way of putting it so that it serves a specific purpose.

Now, if we contrast the Popess in this thinking to the Pope, we can see that while the Pope is invested in counseling precisely on 'the path' and the goal and direction you can take in your life, the Popess is more invested in asking: 'what path?' What words exactly describe this path, and who do these words serve?'

After all, she is the woman of the words. The Pope speaks them in ritual, but he didn't write the words himself. Therefore I say that when it comes to knowing one's purpose, it's best to go to the Popess for an answer, as she'll turn it into art… if she insists on keeping silent, or at the very least, turn into a good story.

BY THE HAIR

Because we're with words and writing here, I'm looking at my trumps for instruction on how I can continue with my deconstructed card of the Popess, as she seems to go in and out of focus, perhaps indeed, embodying the very image of the woman sitting in the chair with a book in her hands, now reading, now staring. I wish I could say that she is thinking, but I can't know that for sure. Staring is staring. If it also involves thinking, it's hard to tell, so we're with a challenge here… until, the Tower.

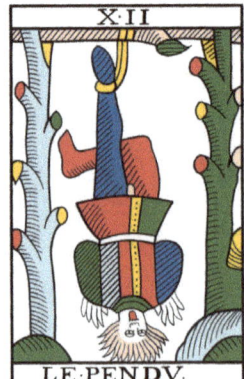

While looking at the Tower, the Priestess, and the Hanged Man, trying to maintain an empty mind of 'no judgment,' I feel my cultural competence kicking in, sending me to the world of enchantments: 'Rapuntzel, Rapuntzel, let down your hair, so that I may climb thy golden stair.'

The Brothers Grimm fairytale about the young damsel with enchanted golden hair locked up in the tower hits on me. The hair is used as a rope for the witch who keeps Rapuntzel away from the world. Whenever she needs to visit Rapuntzel and climb to her chamber, she sings the spell. The spell opens the gate to beauty and richness.

But what if it does more? What if it unlocks fears and desires? What if the spell unlocks the acceptance of the 50/50 rule? Sometimes the witch climbs the golden stairs, and sometimes the prince climbs the golden stairs. Although we know how it all went once the Prince learnt the spell, the truth is that without the witch's 50 percent part in it, creating the spell and maintaining secrecy about it until she got busted, he would never have thought of Rapunzel as being fascinating, worth conquering, and as fulfilling of his deepest desire.

The point here is that any string of cards, whether laid out as a 10-card Celtic Cross or as a 3-card spread, tells a story that can be experienced both spontaneously and as validating of what you already know. As soon as the image hits your eyes, you find the words pouring. Words that describe, analyze, evaluate, and give advice. The image follows the words, always, simply because what makes divination an act of fortunetelling is words, the words that go into formulating in the form of a question what you have in your heart: hopes and fears.

How do you go beyond them? After all, secretly, you also want to be a Zen master, someone who reads cards like the Devil, or who is capable of cutting everything to the bones in one movement.

'Priestess, oh priestess, let down your words so that I may climb thy inky swords.'

The word is sharper than the sword, they say. Perhaps, indeed, what cuts the Hanged Man's rope is the *parole,* the uttered spell, not the blade and not the axe, but the enchantment that will last... that is, if the Prince manages to escape getting hung up by the foot with a rope made by the golden hair that he so desires.

If the worst comes to worst, will the Prince be able to say, 'by my hair, I'll do something about this situation right now,' or will he come to a different realization?

WHEN THE HANGED MAN CAN'T HELP IT

THE HANGED MAN IS NOT ABOUT a different perspective. First and foremost, the Hanged Man is about the inverse of the situation, calling us to consider events and their inverse manifestation.

Thinking of the inverse of any situation we're presented with can teach us something about how to avoid nasty occurrences. Such thinking used to be part of an old Stoic repertoire, with philosophers insisting that it's good to develop a sense of detachment from your desire to achieve something, by always imagining the inverse of the situation. For instance, if you want to climb to the very top of your profession, the practice is to also imagine while climbing what the situation would look like if you failed. What would be the things you'd steer away from? Unless you can imagine the inverse of the success story, it's not very likely that you can learn any tricks of avoidance.

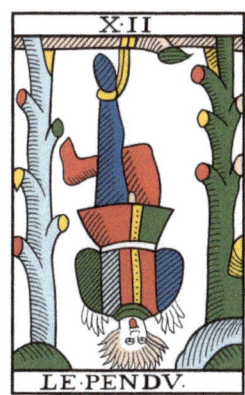

Since the Stoics taught this tactic, it has been used to various degrees in other disciplines and settings, from military strategy and management to concepts such as 'reverse psychology.'

Thinking of the inverse of the situation is also useful when you have to declare things like: 'now they like you, now they don't.' In considering the motivations behind people's change in attitude, if you don't apply the inverse of the situation, you may be tempted to speculate on the 'why'; 'why don't they like me anymore?'

But that is not the most useful when you're dealing with entitlements. Most people's attitudes are polarized: 'yesterday I loved you, today I'm entitled to hate you.' Fair enough. If you're mentally strong and stable yourself, you can even retort: 'be happy on your way. Be judicious. Don't waste my time.'

What I find useful is to look at what lesson the Hanged Man teaches, namely the lesson of acceptance, often captured in this phrase: 'It can't be helped'. Now, most would say that when a situation can't be helped, what it discloses is resignation, the danger also being that with resignation comes resentment. But if we looked at a situation and how it unfolds as a matter of flow, whether we like it or not, we realize that the only proper response to all of it is to say: 'it can't be helped.'

It can't be helped when people hang you by lying about you. It can't be helped when your act of questioning their integrity is deemed an act of projection. It can't be helped when your act of asking for legitimation is deemed an act of refuting criticism. It can't be helped when you point to the injurious insult, and people stupidly ask you: 'what's the big deal?'

Try saying that to yourself, 'it can't be helped,' next time someone hangs you, or you find yourself in an impossible situation. You'll be surprised at your next step.

Mine begins with this realization: 'it can't be helped' is the only condition for the existence of 'keep going.'

GO BEYOND

One of the main points about the Hanged Man in esoteric Tarot is that it's all about renunciation à la Eastern philosophy, where we have the figure of the yogi, kindly accepting his 'fate,' also known as the realization that you come into the world, you live, and you die. You can have an opinion about it, but it matters zero in the face of life happening as it happens.

In this sense the Hanged Man is a representative of the conscious act of going beyond all societal constructions. Historically, however, the Hanged Man has simply referred to a traitor situation, with the traitor being dragged to the main town square, to be 'drawn and quartered,' which is a punishment technique with death as the outcome.

Can we read the Hanged Man as an instance of 'going beyond' as it also connects to the main idea here of acknowledging the situation that can't be helped?

Let me share a personal story again.

SMOKE TRAVEL

When my sister visits we often engage in a ritual of smoking pipes. This is a family tradition that we have inherited from my grandmother on my father's side. The pipe, not the ritual. As the story goes, my grandmother was a woman of her own mind who invested zero energy in her reputation. No woman in the small village of Caian in Transylvanian Romania smoked pipes, but she did.

This woman fascinates me, as she is the 'type' who seems to have been well versed in the beyond: being beyond rules and conventions, beyond prejudice, beyond gossip, and beyond petty drama. My sister and I devised a ritual of convocation, when we imagine that we travel to whereever it is that our grandmother is, so we can all smoke together in the beyond. Just look at us here…

GO, GO, GO BEYOND, GO THOROUGHLY BEYOND

When I think of my grandmother, I actually see her as the embodiment of the famous last line mantra in the Buddhist sacred text called *The Heart Sutra*: 'Go, go, go beyond, go thoroughly beyond. Thus.'

What I like in this text, a text that operates with being in paradox – that to me, at least, equals living the magical life – is the fact that while we have a delineation of three linear stages that lead us to the fourth stage of the beyond, there is no separation between these stages, as they all take place simultaneously with the negation of place and the negation of affirmation.

The first 'Go' has to do with getting a glimpse into how intuition operates beyond the conceptual level, as it is practically a glimpse into awareness beyond agency. For instance, I don't decide to intuit something. I just recognize a phenomenon. Intuition is a way of grasping reality without personal effort going into this grasping.

The second 'go' follows intuition and its spontaneous glimpse into the experience of accepting and embracing what is 'seen' or intuited. The simple interjection 'Ah,' summarizes the whole experience: 'Ah, I see this, I get this.' But seeing it and getting it are also acts of non-deliberate knowledge. That is to say, the 'Ah,' emphasizes the process that goes towards the realization that there's nothing behind the phenomenon of experiencing reality.

This process is further refined by an act of contemplation, the third 'go,' a stage where what is at stake is allowing for curiosity to take over. Those accustomed to sitting in meditation know that after the first initial stages, if we are patient enough and keep going, we arrive at a process of inquiry into the nature of our wonder: what is this 'Ah', and where does it come from?

The final stage of this line of experiencing a glimpse into reality is being in what I like to identify as a state of grace, beyond knowledge and the necessity to explain what is happening. We are beyond the conceptual, descriptive, and reflective level of what is happening. What is happening *is* what is happening. Whether we have an opinion or not about the nature of what is happening, where it comes from and why, and how we can use what we see is happening to further the value of our experience, is completely uninteresting in the grand scheme of the 'Ah' that continues as a pay off and as an anchor in reality. The 'Ah' – beginning the circle and ending the circle – is precisely thoroughly beyond all points of reference and identification.

UNDERGROUND FOLKLORE

While my sister and I have this moment of non-identification with the smoke and the ritual, while we're at it nonetheless and for a very specific purpose, we talk about our roots. We conclude that most of our Romanian folklore is an underground folklore, a folklore of the underworld, a folklore that is not liminal, but of the beyond, a folklore of vampires and screeching owls, dark maidens and night demons. Sometimes I look for Hekate, the

Bearer of the Keys, but in the Romanian context, all I get is Lilith, the Strigoaica, the howler and witch.

'You know,' my sister tells me, while puffing contemplatively on her pipe, 'right now there are only two competing funeral parlors in our home town, Arad, near the Hungarian border. One of them is called Cookie and the other Nosferatu. Imagine the dearly beloved dropping dead, and the family having to make arrangements with the monsters or the undead.'

I'm about to meet my own maker from too much laughter at this innocuous fact, when I realize that, indeed, I can imagine the very thing. Why would the Aradian funeral parlors be about liminality and thresholds? They are all about the beyond already. At this point my smoke takes a swerve, and so do I. I tell my sister that there's a reason why we were both born in Arad, why Aradia, Lilith's other name is our patron by default, why we now live in Denmark, yet curse like gypsies, and why we sit in Zen and Tibetan Buddhist meditation of the Dzogchen orientation, or the kind that places you in the infinite as soon as you snap your fingers. Sister nods in approval. She knows what she knows.

BEYOND HERITAGE

Following the 4 stages of the beyond outlined above, we decided to ask the cards the following: 'what is the best thing about our Aradian heritage?'

The cards that fell on the table were quite miraculous – but then it is a rare occasion when I don't find any configuration of cards miraculous.

Still.

What we got was Death, Temperance, the Hanged Man, and the World. I consciously picked a fourth card after the initial three 'go, go, go,' as an emphasis on the 'thoroughly beyond.' The World showing up in this position, suggesting pure awareness and infinity in this context, was quite auspicious.

PERFECT WISDOM, PERFECT PLAY

Given the nature of our question, upon seeing these cards we realized immediately the perfection of the mantra, 'gate gate pāragate pārasamgate bodhi svāhā,' 'go, go, go beyond, go thoroughly beyond, thus'. The first condition for the existence of any 'beyond' is death. So death comes as a gift, as a preparatory stage for our contemplations.

Temperance stands for the mixing of the 'Ahs' – here quite literally as the final breath – with the other elements depicted on the World card in the corners, which can be the 4 evangelists and their emblems, the 4 cardinal points, or the 4 elements: Air, Earth, Water, Fire. Temperance is a master at making a cocktail, mixing and permuting with all that is already, transforming substance and perception.

The Hanged Man begs the question: Why? Why must the Witch always hang? The answer to this is obvious. Traditionally, all women who knew too much were hanged, one way or another. On second thought, nothing much has changed. A woman's insight is followed by hanging. It can't be helped. We call this reality. Gone beyond, for sure, to the World.

The first 'go, go, go, beyond' can easily translate here into a more contemporary and common mantra that I referred to already: 'Keep going.' Temperance prepares you for it. In the face of being hanged, what is there to do other than to keep going, one way or another? So the best part of our Aradian heritage is that we keep going. I asked my sister, while I enveloped myself in a final smoke: 'was there ever a time when we were not here already, at all these stages simultaneously and precisely in the beyond?' She said, 'no.' I felt at this point that she was echoing my grandmother, who also said 'no,' who, in her own hanging, turned into smoke and vanished into the eternal return of the dark.

The intuition about the beyond, that is not only instantly recognized but also embraced, leads to the kind of curiosity about all things that can easily be perceived as a form of radical acceptance: 'I don't know what this is, but I like it.' In this radical acceptance we are even beyond the sum of all our experiences, intellectual and emotional states. We are with the 'way out there,' which is also here, an instance of 'I'm here now'.

I said to my sister, 'let's curse someone, the one who hangs us'. 'Ah, how good,' she said. 'Let's do just that.'

And so we did.

WHEN TEMPERANCE IS OBSESSIVE

THERE ARE TIMES when Temperance is worse than the Devil. Yes. You heard that right. When Temperance is worse than the Devil is when she encourages obsession. Obsession is in vogue, even to the point where we can argue that, unless you find something to obsess about grand style, it's not sure that anyone will take you seriously.

Why is obsessing about something a good thing? And when does 'good obsession' fail?

I won't talk about the obsession with lost lovers, resentment and hatred, and other such addictions to people and objects, indeed, very much the domain of what we associate with the Devil. I'll talk about the kind of obsession that grants you heavy caliber. Many would swear that what makes you successful, personally and professionally, are basically two things: diligence and concentration. Everyone seems to understand what diligence and concentration are all about. They are about the capacity for endurance and focus. Fair enough. But how do you apply this understanding to the practice of everyday life in a world

where concentration span dwindles faster than the speed of light, with endurance becoming a thing of the past? Athletes are closer to practicing concentration and endurance on a daily basis, but most who are not athletes must settle for the desire for focus and determination, without realizing this desire.

Desire desires desire, and that's the trouble with it. Desire is not 'doing it.' Temperance, in her obsession with her chalices, comes very close to committing the *faux pas* of not realizing that in order for her not to be obsessed the wrong way, she needs to develop meta-awareness of her potential clinging to the idea of concentration and endurance. Desiring mental stability – because it gives you access to discrimination and discernment – is one thing. Obsessing about being a champion at maintaining balance is another. The first has to do with detached desire, the second with desire that generates more desire, thus getting you nowhere.

The subtle lesson of Temperance is this: what you must make a note of, as you try to keep it steady, is the point when obsession kills it. Good obsession kills it perfectly. Just one arrow. Bad obsession overkills.

Temperance is particularly helpful when 'a Lovers situation' is on the table, because ambivalence and not being to able to make up your mind sure overkills it every time. Temperance is also helpful when the Devil has you chained, in the process convincing you that this is something that you absolutely like.

Some in the self-help arts will make a case for indulging your base desires, because supposedly these are the ones that disclose your 'true' power. What do you think that that business about permission is all about? 'Give yourself permission to do this or be this,' 'give yourself permission to do that or be that,' the well-intended will shout from the bottom of their lungs. Alas, this shouting is not an expression of *hara* power, as it's just a show, which, on occasion makes me desire to shout back: 'why don't you give yourself permission to know better, to cultivate discipline, and to show moderation and temperate action?'

Be that as it may. We're not going there, obsessing about the shallow thinkers. The trouble is that base desires are just that, base, and if they generate anything, then it's more desire; desire for shifts, transformations, new identities, and empowerments. Sometimes you wonder where living the simple life is in all this desiring.

For true power you must dig stuff diligently and with a lot of focus. The purpose of this digging is to get you to understand that there's nothing that's important in the world. Gossip and devilish excitement stemming from the insecure that will have you believe in all sorts of things are not important. This is what I said to the person I read the above cards for, who wasn't sure who to listen to. 'Don't listen to the voice of teenagers who think that just because they can throw a tantrum, they're in the know about life and such. If only...'

If you can develop obsession over something *and* at the same time maintain this awareness, that there's nothing that's important in the world, you'll be a champion at clarity, at seeing things as they are. You'll be free from bullshit discourse and tactics whose aim is only to get you deeper into the illusion of how good desiring desire is. A temperate state avoids falling into the Devil's trap of desire, when there's understanding of what is timely, and of how far a personal elastic can be stretched.

Finally, you may want to ask your own cards this question, if you feel the need to check with your diligence and endurance: 'what in my life kills it just perfectly?' My own cards on this question, the Sun, Judgment, and the Hanged Man, had this to say: 'you pick the other according to your own size. You deliver the news, and leave it there.'

At first, I wanted to say, 'oh no, not the Hanged Man again,' thinking of all the hanging situations, when I remembered my curse. It's not about sharing the news with like-minded folks and then expect to be hanged. It's about saying it, and leaving it there. It's about exhaling.

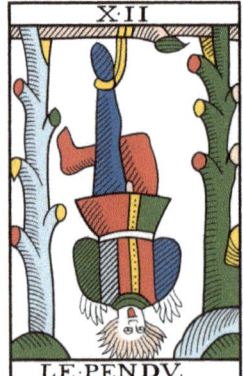

WHEN THE STAR DOES MORE THAN KNEEL

LET'S STAY WITH THE FAMILY for a while longer. My sister visited me from Copenhagen. I asked out of courtesy: 'how are things?' 'I follow the same principle in love and work,' she said. I got curious, as I like principles. The good ones that are more than the manifestation of inflexibility are hard to come by. My sister is good at the good ones. She said: 'at work with my patients at the hospital, I say to them: I'm at your disposal, but not at your discretion. Same thing at home. Then she gave me the squinting eye: 'you must understand the importance of this, as I know you don't appreciate unjustified entitlements either.' Indeed I don't.

This made me think about the cards among the trumps of the Tarot, and how they represent this distinction. Think of how many actually are all about making offerings, giving. Temperance says: 'I'm at your disposal,' while measuring what there's to measure.

What about the Star? It's a more complex card in this relation. You'd think that, unlike Temperance, the Star places herself at the discretion of the others. All that nakedness can easily be mistaken for looseness, for rendering yourself vulnerable, so that others can take advantage.

These days people willingly place themselves at the discretion of others without discernment, because the new story in vogue is that vulnerability is good. Vulnerability is good for whom?

These days I want to blurt: 'spare me the vulnerable act,' whenever I come across conscious embodiments and statements as to the supposed value of vulnerability. But if I said anything of the sort, if I said what I really thought, I'd run the risk of getting lynched. How dare I exhibit such coldness....

Meanwhile, in most standard symbolology, the Star is often associated with making offerings, generosity, and openness to the point of naivety. But all this presupposes an Other at whose discretion the woman in the Star card willingly positions herself. Her gesture, however, discloses that if she's at anyone's discretion, then it's more the discretion of nature. Her own nature.

In meeting your own nature head on, you discover that there's no need for temperance here, for restraint, as disposal and discretion become the manifestation of one. Placing yourself at your own discretion means placing yourself in the highest, when you don't have to make any choices. That's honouring your true nature. I'd kneel for this one myself.

My sister's example above reminded me of the general question that many want to pose to the fortuneteller, when they don't really want to invest any energy in having an encounter with the person they want to know something about. A spying situation. 'How is he doing?' is almost the same as asking your own sister, 'how is everything?' Such questions are non-committal in the sense that there isn't any expectation here as a result of clear projection.

Once such a question was on the table: 'how is he?' a woman wanted to know about an intimate friend she was not currently in touch with. I'm not bothered by such questions, even though I prefer the ones where there's a stake in it. It's fair enough to want to know about somebody, because you happen to think of them. And how fortunate that when you're not ready to talk, pick up the phone, or write the man a letter, you can go to the fortuneteller...

Here's an interesting example of a string of cards, one that invites you to consider the problem with agency, the problem with identifying who is doing what to whom, from whose perspective we perform the reading, and who we ultimately address or talk about. I haven't fully explored this methodical challenge in this book, as I've reserved discussing techniques and mechanics to my introduction books and the teaching of my foundation courses, but this example illustrates a point about precision.

Let's have the question again. 'How is he?' the woman wants to know, in that non-committal way that makes the fortuneteller realize that whatever her answer, it will make little impact.

The Star, the Wheel of Fortune, and the Popess made an appearance. I said: 'he's not doing anything interesting. He's caught in routine, along with a younger and an older woman. He doesn't have much to say in it. The women here have more agency.'

'Yes, it's the wife and his mother,' the sitter said, looking at the cards in a detached and rather sad way.

To make it more interesting, I said the following: 'if you had asked a more specific question, one about this man's relationship, I would have said the following: 'the naked woman got tired of serving, put on some clothes, and got behind the wheel, ruling it by the book.'

'Ah, yes', the sitter said. 'That *is* interesting.' A spark of excitement in her eyes was unmistakable. This story was much better. Shifting the focus from him to one woman was definitely more interesting. After all, we're here with a prominent female cast and no man, expect the tiny king on top of the Wheel of Fortune.

'Why do you think the wife got tired of him?' the sitter then asked, assuming already to know at least half the truth.

'I don't know,' I said, 'maybe because he's too boring, too predictable, going with whatever change is coming. Not all naked women want to keep serving such men, kneeling for them, when all they offer in return is nothing but predictable chores.'

'Ah, yes, not good,' the sitter now said with eerie eyes. I could tell she was thinking about how *she* would handle the situation. Would she also turn cold and let everything be about logistics?

I stopped the conversation before it turned into a dream and gossip about a likely uninteresting person and his predicament.

But it goes to show. The same three cards can tell two very different stories. The art is to stay on track with the question and the right distribution of attention.

CLOTHES ON, CLOTHES OFF

When we talk about seeing the obvious, we talk about seeing everything first. The obvious emerges as a strengthening of what is implicit in the question already. The implicit can be overt or manifest. In the case of the previous question, 'how is he doing?' the implicit is not manifest. By pointing to the observation that the naked woman can get dressed and perform a different job, we received contextual information that we then processed as knowledge.

Of course, we're never with any knowledge based on certitude, least of all when we 'tell fortunes,' when we say many things that are not immediately subject to verification. What the cards do is provide us with what we can term 'fictional truth'[1]. We use words to describe what we see, an internal story in images. Fictions. But the words we use move the other, so we can assume that the words hold some truth for the ones who hear them. In other words, we operate with conjectural knowledge, but often that is enough when it comes to having to make a decision that feels entirely naked and true to us.

Once I made a few comments about the Star and the Sun in the context of one-on-one teaching that I think others reading here might benefit from hearing, especially since I haven't seen anyone else offering similar insights.

It's about intermittence. Clothes on, clothes off. That's what we see in the Sun card, if it's the Marseille Tarot we're working with.

---

1 For a literary study of the paradox of truth in fiction, I recommend Michael Riffaterre's book, *Fictional Truth* (1990).

In the Star card we have a steady stream of nakedness, as it were, mirroring the flow of the river. But also here there's intermittence. Depending on how much disturbance you apply to the surface and density of the water with your outpouring, what we get is reflection on, reflection off.

Have you ever thought of why the people in the Sun card are both dressed and undressed? As yet I haven't heard anyone proposing any interesting theory about it, but in context it seems to me that there's something to it, to the idea of always having an encounter with others either in dressed mode, or in undressed mode.

In the course of our discussion, the student I said all this to had the Magician and the World flanking the Sun. My suggestion was that in the context of assessing the value of an encounter, what one needs to consider is the extent to which now you fake it, and now you don't. That's the beat. Clothes on, clothes off.

As far as the Star goes, the student whose assignment I commented on was discussing the issue of confidence. Yes. There's that. But how many understand confidence beyond theory? If you think about this card, you'll see that it's not only about nakedness and vulnerability. Rather, it is very much also about standing alone and being self-reliant. Many pass the deep understanding of the implications of being self-reliant, simply because not many are ready to face the army of haters who will make sure to hold it against you that you're self-reliant, not needing a community. How dare you not need people? How dare you not need their validations, endorsements, and attitude of 'I like you, and therefore I approve of you. Now say thank you.'

We find the culmination of self-reliance in the World card, as we pointed out earlier, but here's what I think about the same idea where the Star is concerned. What you can get from the Star standing alone, naked, is the type of confidence that's called, 'being in a league of your own.' No evangelists here. It's a good idea to know what that really means. It's also a good idea to know that while there's never any point in comparing – apples and apples, or apples and oranges alike – others will insist on doing it, and you will have to take that into account when you're ready to flaunt being in a league of your own; not in the sense of letting opinions of what you do influence you, but rather in the sense of learning how you position yourself vis-à-vis what's being thrown at you, from sincere feedback to flattery for an agenda, or full blown hatred.

To give an example from the spiritual world that's not very different from the mainstream world of education, everyone is mighty keen on 'rating the professor'. 'This is the best,' 'this other one sucks. I know it because I've tried the other one who was so much better.' While some opinions are justified, others are not.

Now, comments such as these can be helpful and have a function, but the most helpful and unbeatable is to try things for yourself. Read that book that others are talking about for yourself, and make up your mind about it on your own. Take that course and judge its value for yourself. If you don't, you might later come to the conclusion that you've been listening to the wrong channels of communication and you learn that the train has left the station without you onboard – hence you wasted an opportunity. You might also learn that there's a lot of energy that people invest in utter nonsense. But let that be your own judgment. As to loss, indeed, sometimes the book you read is no good, and the course you take is not interesting enough. You may think, 'loss of time and loss of money.' In reality, however, you will have gained knowledge of experience. First hand and entirely your own. This beats being impressionable.

When you're confident à la the Star, what it means is that you're in a league of your own, and always already beyond influence. You can also develop compassion for the ones who will insist on placing what you do in relation to what others do, but then you have to think of your thing as that which has no match, as there are things that only *you* can do. This is a fact.

When the Star shows up in a reading, she invites you to consider what all the kneeling is all about. Sometimes the serving is without a match.

BEYOND COMPARISON

From my own life experience, it never ceases to amaze me, for instance, why people want to compare what I do to what other people do. What is the point? We each mind our business, and although we may have conversations about philosophy or the Tarot, at the end of the day, I will never have any interest in looking anxiously over my shoulder, and try to match what these other people do – often just because some think I should; on the question of authority, it can't be helped that men hold more of it over women, whether such holding is legitimate of not, fair or not. When culture dictates its rules, you can reject them, but it's not sure that with this rejection you can change the world.

I could spend an inordinate amount of time being frustrated over this common attitude, 'yes, you're good, but I still have to think about you.' Instead I choose to see the reality of what I do, and the fact that what I do has absolutely no match. Others may want to compare, but let that be their loss of breath. This doesn't mean that what I do that has no match is better or worse than what others do. It simply means that if something has no match, then it has no match. Your thing is your thing. As such, how can it compare? That is the plain obvious, and I prefer to stick to it, rather than get emotional about it.

The card of the Star invites us to consider how the woman here has internalized such knowledge, and because of it she keeps going her way, doing her thing, enjoying being in her own league. Confidence doesn't mean being comfortable with your nakedness, but rather, being comfortable with being in a league of your own.

In contrast, the Sun card features two people on it who know their place and who know when it's appropriate to have an encounter with their clothes on and when they can afford to have them off. Being in a league of your own means having distinction that you apply to yourself first.

When the Star does more than kneel, is when she suddenly realizes that the emptying of her chalices is a perfect mirroring of the act of emptying herself of all that doesn't serve her. Such awareness is not naïvety, even though any act of emptying may come across that way – when people go and refer to others being empty in their heads, they don't mean it as a compliment.

In mundane questions, when the Star poses the question, 'who am I really?' emptying herself of all the surrounding fictions, she does not ask this question with view to answering it. That is something that the Hermit as a philosopher might do. The Star merely asks the question and doesn't expect an answer to arise. She simply abides in her nakedness. Such nakedness is the representation of perfect silence, and is therefore the highest.

Do we love her for it? Yes, we do, but not if what we want from her is her submission. Therefore the question, 'does he love me?' cannot always be answered in the affirmative, if the Star is followed by the Emperor. The Star doesn't mean 'hope,' any more than the Emperor means 'stability.' She means what she means, a naked woman enjoying the starry night, not caring about love.

WHEN THE DEVIL IS CRYSTAL CLEAR

CLARITY IS A RARE COMMODITY. As far as I'm concerned, the number one enemy of clarity is the following string: projection, denial, worry, aversion, resentment, hatred, competition. The string is long, but let's just say, these are things culturally associated with the Devil. I'm not in the camp of those who think that the Devil in the Tarot is good news. It's not. Let's see what I mean.

In questions that call for advice, given the general ambiguity of the Devil card – now it's about passions and underground design, now it's about nasty obsessions – we can be tempted to say things like this in a reading session: 'it's a good idea to manipulate and lie if you want to stay alive.'

If you're a person of strong moral principles, you're going to resist 'doing' the Devil, or doing the Devil's bidding, even if the Devil's strategy may well be to your advantage. So how can you avoid the detrimental situation, or rather, how do you read the Devil when it's in the position of advice?

Do we go with the idea of 'doing' the Devil? Or do we go with the idea that when the Devil is in the picture, whatever context we're dealing with, we must cut it all out; cut out the lies, the immoral strategizing, the pretense, the shifting masks of identity, and so on.

In principle, which option you go for is entirely up to you. If the Devil is sometimes good news for you, then you can indulge the liberty to suggest to your sitter that doing devilish things is in order, or at least a good idea.

If you're thick in the head and insist on doing judicious things, like me, then, whenever you'll see the Devil in your readings you will know that compromise is not what you will advise. You pass judgment, 'do the Devil,' and you leave it at that.

Here's an example of one such reading. I got this question based on a context that required clarity – a classic, really, as I'm presented with this situation all the time. Says the querent: 'there's something that's missing, as I have a hard time figuring out what's most pressing and important that I must do connected to my work. What is this thing that's both urgent and significant at the same time? Three cards fell on the table: The Emperor, the Moon, and the Devil.

I said the following in a tirade: 'it's urgent that you consider what exactly you have to offer. What is this one thing that you're all about? What's your tag line, your emblem? Try to consider what that thing is beyond what you imagine is a good idea, thus projecting what you think the others want. While you're at it, figuring it out, can you also please be honest about it? Don't sell yourself a fantasy, thus putting yet another layer of darkness over your one thing.

Even if you don't like it, make sure that selecting the one thing is the most urgent. Hold that scepter up, so you can see clearly what you yourself already inscribed on it.

It's significant that you don't disregard the one thing, whether you like it or not, in favor of the attitude, 'let me add more creativity to it,' because you happen to second-guess the other due to your desire to either manipulate or hide your insecurity because you're afraid.

If you have to deep-dive, make sure you follow your strategic map, or else you'll never get out of the pool of mud. You may be tempted to play a power-game, but unless you're prepared for hell, I wouldn't advise it. Just choose your focus, throw your fishnet, and wait. Sooner or later you'll get something on the hook.'

TAKE TWO

This type of advice above would have looked entirely different, had I chosen to see the Devil as a good thing to do, such as, lying a little about concentrated power, or bending the general integrity at stake.

If I say to people 'do the Devil,' what I actually mean is this: pay attention to where the Devil appears (initial, middle, final position in a 3-card layout), and then note how the Devil's primary function to distort reality actually fits in with clarity.

Only on rare occasions did it make sense for me to say to the other that accepting the bondage was a good idea at the time.

You can think of the Devil as someone to imitate, but you can also think of the Devil as a red flag.

As far as I'm concerned, the Devil calls me to one thing only, namely, to exorcise the hell out of all the demons that afflict and possess. I read cards for clarity, not for participating in dubious undertakings. When the Devil shows up, I don't negotiate.

WHEN THE TOWER IS A TAG

NOT ONCE, BUT SEVERAL TIMES people have complained that in my readings of the cards I was not being very supportive of their desires. I have a problem with 'supportive' – not to mention desire – because I'm not sure what it means. Does being supportive mean being 'sympathetic,' 'empathetic,' 'participating in healing and growth,' 'validating,' 'listening and nodding,' while my judgment is suspended or not so suspended? What do all these concepts and attitudes mean? Just the thought of it gives me a headache already.

Here's an example where I used a very efficient 5-card draw. The first 3 cards down described the situation. The card on top said, 'do this,' and the card at the bottom said, 'avoid this.' So this layout is a combination of the method of reading the first three cards in line coupled with the two additional positional readings, with each of the two cards designating the 'meaning' of the place: 'do this,' and 'don't do that.'

I was reading for a person who wanted to know whether it was the right time for her to teach herbalism.

The cards said, 'do the Hermit and don't do the Pope.' So I said, 'do the Hermit, think some more, and don't do the Pope. You're not ready to teach.' The Tower was also in the picture, following Force and the Moon, thus announcing a sure disaster after struggle with not seeing clearly.

This was pretty clear talk to me. In its clarity this talk was neither supportive nor non-supportive. It was what it was: it pointed towards making a realization. Nonetheless, since this was not the 'right' answer, I got it thrown in my face that I was not being supportive and that I was messing with the person's peace of mind. I also got blocked as a friend on Facebook, as if my virtual presence there was a contamination of this person's life and goals. I don't want to say that this behavior is new to me, as I've seen worse, but I see what motivates it.

People see other people in the spiritual business as belonging to what they imagine is the 'supportive community'. The supportive community is also imagined to be everything that the competitive community is not. We're here with the assumption that one community is holier than the other. We're here with the idea that spiritual folks are not competitive, but serving by validating. We're here with the idea that there's support in validation.

The question that now begs itself is this: Is this really so? People like to share their shattering and vulnerable stories because that makes them feel less alone in their experiencing life's vicissitudes. But is saying, 'I feel sorry for you,' supportive in any way? How? I fail to see what substance 'I feel sorry for you' has. How can empty words and fillers move anyone? Some would say, it's a way of being present for the one who has a hard time. I'm not convinced, as I don't see how empty words can fill a space.

UNDERSTAND WISELY, NOT IMAGINE VIVIDLY

As far as I'm concerned, you're supportive when you have a clear understanding of another person's situation. But how can we have a clear understanding of another person's situation when we're not in it?

Some would say, 'well, people tell you the story of their life, and that's how you understand.' Maybe so, but it seems to me that understanding problems based on stories all too often leads to shallow thinking and shallow conclusions. The point I'm trying to make here is actually this one: if there's a major fear that the spiritual community suffers from, then it's this one, everyone fears that they are not supportive enough.

But supportive of what? How does the supportive manifest? Look around. How many times have you seen a spiritual community whose tower doesn't get smashed at least once a day? Facebook is a great example of this. Look around for the 'supportive' dynamics in a group. It only takes about 5 minutes to see who rides what horses and in whose names. Sometimes all three, the riders, the horses, and the names, have a rather dubious character.

It's often the case that what we quickly learn about 'learning communities' is that the 'supportive' is all about who is to be master. On occasion learning does occur, and inspiration can be at hand. But more often than not, the opposite is true. Proclamations are passed on as 'the thing itself,' knowledge is passed on as understanding when it's not, and ideas are passed on as original, when they are not. The dominant dominate, the weak are stunned, being caught in a perpetual state of non-differentiating, and the neutral let it go, indulging in the realization that you can't be critical of the 'supportive' community.

THE MEDDLING CURSE

There can be many reasons why institutions, groups, and communities go bust or experience a lot of trouble. I find that chief among the tensions that lead to destruction is meddling informed by misunderstanding what being supportive is all about. It's not about meddling. To be sure, meddling is not always explicit, as it's often wrapped up in a cloth called 'concern,' but it is nonetheless the cause for many a miserable situation.

Sometimes meddling is downright desired. When others tell you that you're not being supportive, often what they're really saying is that they'd like you to meddle some more in their lives, as this would mean that you'd be more invested in their craving for attention. As I can't imagine any type of meddling having any beneficial aspect, I'll propose this instead: imagine what might happen if people saw their individual roles in whatever community as having to do more with minding one's own business, and less with following, listening to gossip, or giving in to the fear that if one didn't support the views and opinions of a dominant voice, than one would have no identity to adhere to.

As for competitiveness and its supposedly bad name: look at your most favorite spiritual leaders in your corner of the spiritual community. I bet they are competitive and have zero desire to meddle in other people's affairs. They influence through results, not through talking about results. It's impossible not to be competitive when you want to be the best at what you have to offer. Support comes secondary to that.

Being the best at what you do doesn't mean being non-supportive of others who also want to be the best at what they do. Generally, if people exercise their basic capacity for discernment, they can recognize competence beyond proclamations. If people feel supported in their beliefs through your acts, it's wonderful, but the starting premise for a successful delivery of a message is and always will be of a competitive nature first, and then of a supportive character. What you compete with is yourself. When your skills are improved you can be of support to others.

Thus we could say that what we operate with when we transact with our ideas or artisan craft is vivid imagery and subtle suggestion. A vivid image is neither supportive nor competitive. A subtle suggestion is neither honest nor dishonest. An assumption is neither transparent nor opaque. Image and suggestion are just that, image and suggestion free of tags.

Knowing what tower you operate with and from, and taking it at face value, has far more beneficial consequences for your acts and experiences than deciding that a tower that's tagged with an endorsed label is also real. A tag is not a representation of reality.

Communities come with a tag: the spiritual is often tagged with 'supportive' while the corporatist is tagged with 'competitive,' but it will serve you well to know that once you buy whatever the tower sells, you can remove the tag and evaluate the content for yourself beyond others' opinions about it.

If I should give any advice in tackling the shattering towers, it would be this: mind your own business to the best of your ability and in accordance with your basic human decency. Exercise some of that discernment that you possess, that you can also discover you possess when you let yourself be uninfluenced by the voices in the tower. Listen to your own common sense. Believe nothing, and keep going.

What makes you supportive is participating in seeing things as they are, and standing your ground in that positioning.

WHEN THE FOOL IS AN IDIOT

THERE ARE MANY THINGS that people have been saying about the Fool in the Tarot. The list is long, and the meanings and stories assigned to the Fool range from short to tall. Some very tall.

Tradition calls him an idiot. Esoteric approaches to the Tarot see the Fool as a representation of ultimate freedom. This is correct to the extent that the Fool *is* an idiot, but when we think of how esoteric Tarot is not so fond of the idiot *as* a regular idiot, pushing him upwards to the rank of idiot savant, we understand just what is so unsettling about the Fool.

Most also like to think of the Fool as a representation of being on a journey. But why only the Fool? As far as I'm concerned, all the figures of the major arcana of the Tarot can be said to be on a journey.

The Fool follows his path. Aren't we all? We may think we do things contrary to our nature and our true desires, following paths that are not ours. In reality this is not so. We all do the things we do because we're all subject to all sorts of conditions. We walk the path we walk because it is thus. We're part of the flow of nature, not something culturally special, at the center of the universe, acting on free will and all the other fancy stories we tell ourselves.

Given this frame of thinking, I actually often wonder: what exactly do we presuppose when we associate the Fool with freedom and with journeys? I'm not a fan of the Fool, simply because I don't see any value in being utterly unaware, and lacking self-reflection. As a Zen inclined person, while I can appreciate the idea of 'relax and live in the now,' relaxing and living in the now is only possible if you take control of your mind. The Fool has no such capability.

I'm fine with the Fool as a mere idiot. I don't expect anything from him, to inspire me or to frighten me. After all, who can have a relationship with the Fool? I give the Fool due kindness, or the kindness I'm capable of, and that's that. I asked the cards: what is the Fool like? The Hermit, the Charioteer, and the Devil answered clearly: 'the Fool is not unlike a monk, living in the now, stripped of possessions. The only difference is that whereas the Hermit lets go of it on purpose, the Fool is clueless. No awareness. Just drive. Getting straight into all sorts of bondage.

On the other hand, if there's any awareness, then it's followed by a conscious decision: 'I'm so out of here.' The Hermit would say that about the constraints of society, and he might even muster just the energy for it. But unless he sticks to the detachment program, he'll find himself attached again. It's simply not enough to say, 'I'm splitting', only so that you can embrace the lord of demons. The Fool in this manifestation is very bad news.

It occurs to me that when we say, 'you can't fool me,' what we're actually saying is related to bondage: 'you can't bind me with lies.' What do you say when the Fool pops up in your readings? I tend to dismiss him, or tell the others I read the cards for to get away from the Fool as fast as they can. When the Fool is on the table, he disrupts all orders of things.

If the Fool follows his own path, it's a path of errors. In Zen parlance, there's no such thing. There's just people doing people things. But culturally speaking, oy veh. People are not Zen.

The Fool as an inspiration? No thanks. A Fool that talks? I'm so out of here.

JUST SHUT UP

Sometimes I play games in the social media. One of my friends and former student in Aradia Academy's *Nonreading* program asked this question for everyone to answer: 'To end a fear, you have to face it. True or false?'

Amazing answers from people, the majority tilting towards 'face it.' In other words, the majority went for 'true.' I got in the game too and said this: 'fear is a concept like everything else. Dissolve the concept and you're free. Facing this and that is the false consciousness dictating.'

As soon as I wrote that I thought this to myself: 'shut the fuck up. There's a lot of pleasure in most people dissecting concepts or consuming them, not dissolving them. What's the point of going against this pleasure, ruining it for people, or some people anyway, when clinging is here to stay? Not nice.'

On second thought, however, this also made me think of how I deal with the world at large. I listen, I observe, I learn, I engage my curiosity, and pass judgment without judgment. I'm afraid of 'the Fool situation.' I try to have a rigorous practice of discerning, though I may as well disclose that this discerning often happens against the backdrop of dissolving all concepts. I take a lot of pleasure in that to the point where I have to remind myself to put it down, and not attach to it. Whenever I see that my pleasure begins to take over, I send it to hell. 'No attachment, back to zero, back to the void.' This practice serves me well.

BEING COOL WITH CRITIQUE

Here's an example of a reading for someone who kept complaining about doing what I do, deconstruct language and its fictions, but not being cool about it afterwards. Oh, the clinging to guilt, lots of pleasure right there. A bad one...

'What if I'm wrong in my attitude?' this person asked most sincerely. 'What if I'm merely critical, not discerning?' Indeed, it's a fair question to ask, especially since seeing things as they are can be confused with claiming that you do, when in reality you don't. How to know the difference?

If you're not ready to dissolve all concepts – usually that settles everything beyond any negotiation or dispute – looking at a string of cards can give you an idea.

In questions about what attitude to embody vis-à-vis a situation that seems beyond resolve, the reading must follow the rule of imparting advice all the way through the cards. Here, the Pope, the Fool, and Death, suggest what is left when the impossible situation arises. The cards say: 'just shut up. Not all fools get it. You can't save them all with a blessing.'

To make it easier to understand why it's not always beneficial to read the cards from the standpoint of giving, or finding diplomatic solutions – here I could have said, 'just admonish the Fool without reservation, as he'll come to his demise on his own since he never listens – I refer you to a passage in Nisargadatta's work, *Seeds of Consciousness*.

This passage speaks mercilessly of what we make of what we're doing, what gods we worship and why, inviting us to move beyond the urge to say anything, do anything, or think anything.

He says the following in one of his regular *satsangs,* the sitting with the master for a public discourse, where questions are asked and answered:

Q: There are many students of Kundalini Yoga, of Shakti; does the Jnani [sage] necessarily through his practice, through his being, awaken the Kundalini that others speak about?

Maharaj: The Jnani has no interest whatsoever in the Kundalini. Prior to your birth where was the Kundalini? This Kundalini is all that you perceive, all that you see. They call it by different names, that's all.

Q: But some Yogi concentrate a force which goes through the seven chakras and presumably follow the spinal column.

Maharaj: What you say is correct, but prior to your birth it was not there. It is only thought.

Q: Are they all deluded, then, in pursuing the study of Kundalini Yoga?

Maharaj: Anyone who wants to practice anything can do so, but what is it? Zero – Nothing.[1]

DEMYSTIFY AND THEN SHUT UP

Needless to say, part of my own preaching in my work with cards and Zen and nondual awareness draws on such demystifications. It always comes across as 'tough luck' whenever I have to point out that what we call 'truth' and 'reality' has mighty little to do with either truth or reality. Any designation of any idea or phenomenon in words follows cultural conventions. Cultural conventions are just that, conventions, not reality. In the face of an impossible situation, which believing in things always is, the only commonsensical thing to do is to assess what's left to be said. If there's any reality, then this holds true: You simply cannot argue with believers. People will believe in the food that they eat,

---

1 *Seeds of Consciousness*, 1982, p. 110-111.

as they will believe in their gods. You can try to invade 'the sacred,' and you'll see what happens. A sea of fools.

What's left then? To just shut up. You encounter what you encounter, the life you witness, on terms that are completely shared not divided. That's the awesome part. When you encounter fools, keep your tongue. Others will cross your path with a different agenda than to cling to whatever belief.

As my student pondered on my reflections above, she consequently asked: 'How does one dissolve a concept?'

I said, in true Nisargadatta style: 'you dissolve it by being a witness. By saying: fear is what? Zero, nothing at all. The same applies to every other concept on the planet, and that includes, love, children, realization, self-empowerment, the whole long list.' What's left? To witness your attachment to concepts. This will enable you to just shut up and be cool about it without any effort.

NOT THE FOOL'S EASY-GOING

On the question of how you know the difference between critique and discernment, let me make a wider arching comment here on the surprising reason why you read cards to begin with. Easy-going. That's the reason. Not easy-going fun – there's tons of fun in reading cards, and you all it know already – but easy-going in the sense of acceptance: when there's nothing to say, just shut up... You accept that.

What is surprising about reading cards is that they say: take it easy and keep going. The 'take it easy part' is important, as it allows you to understand that although you may read cards to get to the bottom of things – to strategize for a better relationship at work or at home, to be creative in your projects, to find your path and settle goals – in reality, when you read cards you want to learn how to take it easy so that you keep things together and in balance, as balance is the only condition for your resilience.

It's already a given that you can't keep going without resilience. Resilience is not fun. Therefore, you need to take it easy if you're to keep your peace of mind. If you think about it, the whole set of the major arcana contains an embedded message: there are things you can do something about, and there are things you can't do anything about.

There's a surprising subtlety in the cards that says, 'there's nothing you can do here,' or 'it can't be helped; it is as it is.' When there's nothing you can do, and things can't be helped, you might as well take it easy. When you take it easy, you're in accepting mode. When you're in the accepting mode, you're in control of your mind. When you're in control of your mind, you work with your biggest asset, your God-given brain and common sense. When you work with your common sense you can discriminate, and thus respond correctly to any situation.

The value of discrimination is the same as saying yes and no to the right things, without mixing the levels. As an example of the contrary situation, just think about how many times you've read the cards with view to remedy having said yes to the wrong things, and having said no to the right things, 'the Fool situation.'

The realization of having been wrong is always nasty, and it prompts you right there with the challenge of having to admit that it's never about the situation itself, but rather about the way in which you respond to it, and hence, take it easy. So the surprising part, that you're not always aware of, is that you read cards not only for guidance and inspiration, but rather for a clear message on easy-going.

POWER TO ACT

I often say in my cartomantic teachings that one of the most significant distinctions to make in a reading session is the one that discriminates between the cards that afford you a position to act, and the ones that don't. If we talk about the Marseille cards, then think of the ones that afford you no power: the Tower, the Wheel of Fortune, the Hanged Man, Death, the Devil, the Moon, and Judgment. Almost a third of the 22-card pack.

As we've already been through almost all the trump cards, let us deconstruct some more, precisely here in this section about the Fool, so that we end up hammering on what we can avoid, namely, thinking foolishly about that which already presents itself as easy-going. To be clear, no one is to blame for thinking the opposite of what I have to offer. One learns what one learns. But the whole scope of this book is to draw your attention to this question, 'why not, why not think like this too,' in addition to the question that should be the premise for any card reading already, namely, 'why is this so, where does the idea for this particular association come from?'

So far I've made a case for direct experience, but now I want you to consider where your immediate response to the cards comes from, especially if you're familiar with the Tarot in whatever expression, from the standard decks, such as the Waite/Smith Tarot, to the Thoth Tarot, and the Marseille Tarot. Art Tarot can also be part of this list.

WHAT DO YOU SEE?

What do you think when you see these cards, the Hanged Man: 'I can see things differently,' or Death: 'I can now transform,' or Judgment: 'I can go public with my life,' or the Wheel of Fortune: 'I can change,' or the Devil: 'I can be passionate in my seductions,' or the Moon: 'I can be creative?'

To all of this, what I have to say is this: think again. This is even more significant when you use a layout that has the cards locked in specific positions that call for action.

When the Tower is in the position of advice, 'Do this,' do you think that you can *do* the Tower? Blow up like it? You can't. Why? For the simple reason because here the agent is a natural, not a human law. We're here with a natural catastrophe. Lightning hits. If you think you can do anything about a natural catastrophe, you're a fool. So what's the logical thing to infer, then? We can quickly agree that acceptance is the only sensible thing to do. On rare occasion you may enjoy an outburst because it turns out that such a response is appropriate, but this is, as I said, rare.

If it's about your finances and the Tower is in the position of advice, then you can say this to yourself or the other you read the cards for: 'you can become financially stable, if you 'lose' everything you think you know about banks. They're going down.' The same applies to the gambling on the stock market: 'do you speculate? Stop it. The stocks are going down.'

The same applies to Death. You don't fight it. You accept it. You can fight it, but as obvious wisdom teaches us, death wins. So you can forget about fighting. If Death calls you to action, then how do you read it? As a situation whose premise starts with the first personal pronoun in the proclaiming mode, 'I can do this?' If you're lucky, you may be allowed to participate in the wielding of the blade, 'I, the samurai,' but you'll never be the ultimate master.

The same applies to the Wheel of Fortune. You're caught in it. You may think you have agency, but in reality you don't. You're subject to conditions that are external to your own power. Is the Hanged Man in the position of advice? Then wait it out and hope to God that rescue is coming, because if it doesn't, you'll be out of this world. Whether you can see things differently or not, while you're hanging there, is really besides the point when it's about survival. If anything, the Hanged Man says, 'don't die yet.'

When the Moon comes in the position of 'Do this', the more commonsensical thing to do is go to bed and pray for a good dream. You can't bank on being creative when it's plain as daylight that you're not on the same page with others, due to a whole lot of howling and misunderstanding.

When the Devil is in the picture, let's not even go there. You'll think you have agency, but in reality you will have none. Your own obsessions, addictions, resentments, and hatred will have power over you. You won't even be able to see it.

As for Judgment, we're here with the public opinion. Oh, dear. When the trumpet in vogue blasts: 'rise,' most will simply follow, thinking, 'here's the new awakening, we're all individuals.'

THE ART OF ACCEPTANCE

If you think about all this, you get to the surprising lesson that says: 'take it easy! Learn what acceptance is all about.' Acceptance is the attitude that not many consider when reading their cards, because everything has to be so pro-active, but acceptance is there as a very fine, ultimate wisdom: 'you can only keep going, if you take it easy.' If you think about getting pro-active about that, you'll be extending the Fool's function to disrupt everything to where this disruption becomes a conscious busting of habitual patterns. Think about what I've done here, write so many words, when I also said that it's best to shut up. If you find it provoking, I'll say, 'take it easy.'

Take it easy also if you think that you have to memorize 'meanings' in order to perform a competent card-reading. Look at what I've done here so far. I went against the tyranny of 'the secrets of the Tarot revealed.' I simply looked at what we encounter in our daily lives, and considered what questions we can expect to answer.

Now go spread the news about how the cards show you when you have power to act, and when it's best to acknowledge that you don't. Only shut up if the Fools are present, seeing nothing, hearing nothing.

Meanwhile, keep the words, flowing. Keep going.

WHEN JUDGMENT IS ABOUT ALTERNATIVE HISTORY

THE POINT OF FINALIZING this book occurred while on vacation on top of a mountain in Norway. For 20 years I've been spending all my summers in Norway on the mountain plateau for two reasons: 1) the high altitude air, and 2) no tourists. On occasion, however, it happens that the owners of the scattered cabins rent their place to noisy families. This time around, the cabin on the lower slope featured two such families, totaling also 10 children, from baby age to teen age. They were all testing my Zen mind very hard. I was smack in the middle of the 'Judgment card situation,' meaning, my ears were inundated by decibels, witnessing the circus of packing and unpacking cars, loud play, shouting, and begging: 'won't you keep quiet,' the parents would say, to no avail. While the esoteric Tarot school sees this card as a representation of the Last Judgment, awakening, and fast change, in classical fortunetelling Judgment has been associated with 'family.' I can see why. Visually, we're here with the family grave and tradition, the

subtle message being this one: 'we broadcast our values and belief thus.'

As a person who takes a radical stance against all belief, you can imagine how much I like this card... With Judgment in mind, represented on all levels, from the literal to the symbolic, I thought of strategies that would afford me some comfort and power in the face of 'it can't be helped.' In addition to exorcising the noise demon through writing about it here, I retorted to the art of prediction. I performed several divination sessions of predictive character pertaining to the large family's daily activities. I used for it all the cards I'm proficient in reading with, playing cards, Lenormand cards, and Tarot cards of various design. I particularly liked to predict timing, trivial things such as, 'will these people go up the mountain today before lunch?' After some 9 days on the Friday, I asked the cards, 'will these people leave this place tomorrow?' Saturday being a day of shifting cycles. I got these cards: The Tower, the Hanged Man, and Judgment. 'The horror, the horror, of course I got Judgment,' I thought to my self, 'in the final position too...'

 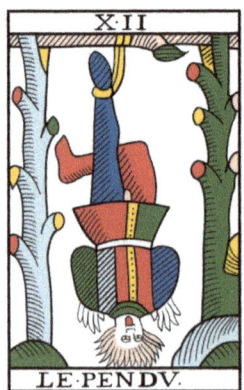 

I predicted that while there will be some commotion disrupting the house, no one was going anywhere, the noise staying. Saturday morning came, and I was curious to see if and how my prediction would come to pass. I heard the noise of the vacuum cleaner. In the context of vacation, this sound normally means that you're done, you're ready to leave. I got excited, but I couldn't help thinking that the Hanged Man in the middle position was not a good sign. As it turned out, the cleaning came and went. The family stayed.

If I wrote a book of card meanings, I'd add this insight to my list: 'the Tower means cleaning the house, the Hanged Man means hanging the laundry, and Judgment means you're fucked.'

ALTERNATIVELY...

I'm looking at these cards, Pope, Judgment, and Temperance, and an odd idea befalls me. Judgment is about alternative history. When we say that this card is about revelation or awakening, what are we really talking about? Alternative history.

In a way all resurrection stories are about waking up to a new reality. But in quantum physics parlance, the 'new' reality is not new at all, as it's been there all along.

I would like to see the Popes of the world stressing the idea that we live in a world of illusion. Our language, name, fate, gods, and will-power are all part of a system that maintains the dream of self as separate from the dreamer. What a waste...

But even as I say this, I realize that here's only so much preaching you can do. People will do what they will do, and most don't even like it at all that you tell them what to do. So I won't say a word, especially since I'm in no 'believer camp' advocating for a 'new dawn,' or for what is right or wrong.

If I have a wish at all, then it's the wish that people see how alternative realities and histories can be mixed up in all sorts of ways, especially since they are not even separated from what we call ordinary reality. Healing from deep wounds in the soul, or from any kind of physical trauma, can occur if you realize that there are at least two versions of *you* that exist concomitantly: one that dies and one that awakens to a new life; one that loses and one that wins; one that loses and wins at the same time; and one that wins and loses at the same time. In other words, you're surrounded by alternative histories of the present. The big awakening is to make that realization.

Part of the occult lore has already acknowledged this, and we see that a lot of discourse draws on knowing and understanding what the higher self has to say and what the unconscious has to say. What we call magic has already been established as being all about honing your conversational skills with all that we call 'the spirit world,' the higher or alternative self, in other words, your deep mind.

I myself play a game with my cartomancy students that involves divining for what the self on the path not taken has to say. For my own entertainment, I also divine a lot for the alternative history of historical events. My favorite genre is the Japanese warring era between 1467-1603.

For instance I asked the cards once: What would have happened if Oda Nobunaga, the first general to attempt the unification of Japan, would not have been assassinated in 1582, in a very strange and idiotic fraction of a second, twist of fate?

I got the Star, the Emperor, and the Lovers answering.

The cards said: Oda Nobunaga would have ruled as the grand man of vision that he was, pursuing his dream of eradicating the court and elevating the strong Samurai to the absolute top position. Alas, however, his subalterns would have been forever vacillating, thus failing to see the big picture.'

You may try to ask your cards similar questions, bearing in mind that any revelation carries the seed of the alternative story or history within it.

205

If Nobunaga came to me for advice, based on his cards here, I would say to him that what he needs is to make his vision crystal clear to the others, so that the possibility for misunderstanding and doubt would be minimized.

In a way he died precisely because of the fact that he gave up on the many and settled with just three who understood what he was all about. He lost patience with the ones who didn't get it, and they got him instead. Nobunaga's vassal, the one who committed the act of treason, couldn't tolerate an Emperor who valued skills more than heritage, in the process plotting to get rid of the real Emperor. In the end, 'tradition' was served by history.

The advantage of posing questions about alternative events or paths or courses of action is that it gives you insight into what you can tweak in your current attitude towards life. If you need more patience, or a strategy that enhances your magnanimity, what would you do? Where would you start? The cards can give surprising and not so surprising answers. Take these answers and merge them into the story of you, now containing also the story of what you could have been, or might be in the future.

There's isn't any separation between these versions, other than the one in your own head. Therefore the practice here is one of enlarging your field of vision so that it encompasses all of you: the past you, the present you, and the future you.

What if Justice informs you all the way through, stuck on the true self and nothing but, or the Devil suppresses your alternative selves, or enslaves you to them, or Temperance mixes up your various selves, thus creating a third mind? Would you even know the difference? A flash of insight into your alternative history can change your path entirely. It can wake you up to new discovery and wholeness.

WHEN THE POPE IS NOT ARROGANT

I'VE BEEN IN THE TEACHING BUSINESS for more than 20 years. Of the 20 years as tenured professor with the university, 10 I've also dedicated to teaching cartomancy and Zen. Since I quit the university, yet still do the latter, I now have more time than before to observe what happens in spiritual and occult circles. I come across this line quite often: 'I'm not a guru. I don't have all the answers,' offered as a means to disperse any potential threat.

More explicitly, here's what I hear: What is presupposed in this statement is 1) that a guru is a con man, and 2) that when a guru says 'it's like this', it's arrogant.

But let me ask you this here: in light of the meaning of the word guru, teacher, and in light of the fact that, when you teach, you teach from a core principle that often *is* totalizing, what can we conclude? We can conclude that what we find in the statement, 'I'm not a guru, I don't have all the answers,' is that there's attachment to false modesty and detachment.

As long as you teach, and as long as your teaching is anchored in what can be termed a universal truth, then the simple fact is that you *are* a guru and you *do* have all the answers.

As it pertains to the idea of not having all the answers, let me give myself as a concrete example. In my teaching I teach from a core principle that rests on investigating into what is just and what is judicious. I don't need moral philosophy to teach me the difference between right and wrong. Connected to this, now think: if you're in a battle and the enemy retreats, you don't immediately take the opportunity to stab the irritating army in the back. That wouldn't be right. In this sense, if I were to teach warfare where this kind of justice is concerned, I'd find that I *do* have all the answers. What is just is just in all situations. It's not like justice is negotiable, so that settles it.

If justice, clarity, or compassion is a principle you build your arguments on, then all your answers will manifest that conviction. If your actions reflect that conviction, then it's because you obviously have all the answers pertaining to your standpoint. You either know what you're doing, or you don't.

Look at the Popes of the world. Don't dismiss them on grounds of arrogance. Teaching what you know with conviction is not arrogance. Defending the precious idea or principle against what doesn't work is not arrogance. It is holding your ground without apology.

If you yourself teach, don't be so quick with your guns, unless it's your own false modesty you want to kill. If you teach, teach. And if you know something essential of this totalizing character: 'It is so,' then say so. Fearing that others might think of you as arrogant, especially if you are strong on your position, is almost as unfortunate as fearing your own total freedom; the freedom that does not have you attached in any way to any perception, object, idea, or projection.

Just teach, and if others call you a guru, say thank you.

HOW THE TAROT WORKS

I asked the cards to give me a topic to write about for this final trump, the Pope. I got some interesting cards, but not ones that surprise me. The Tower, the Devil, and the Hermit suggest that I write about how the Tarot works.

Given what I've been doing so far, dismantling a few established notions, invoking reading like the Devil, and then channeling some mean hermits who have a habit of always talking back, saying, 'you don't say,' as soon as you present something that you want to determine is 'knowledge,' I could say that this topic has already exhausted itself. If it weren't for the Devil calling again, and the Hermit questioning again, I would seal the busted house, and put a sign on it too: 'No trespassing.' As it is, however, here comes a sermon, one I actually gave in variations before.

As many ask about how the Tarot works, and what makes the cards turn up so aptly, enabling us to give answers in a very prompt and concrete way, I've added my own contribution to the lot in various forms throughout the years. But given the cards on the table here, I'll answer this question by making reference to two perceptions and positions we adopt when we approach the cards, either as readers or as seekers ourselves. The first is related to *dual* perception and the second to *nondual* perception.

DUALISM

From the perspective of duality there's the idea – physical and metaphysical – that there's polarity in the world: the Sun and the Moon, Man and Woman, Above and Below. Much of what we call cartomancy comes from our concerns with planetary movements and the desire to read our fate in the stars: 'will she love me tonight?' Fair enough.

In this perspective, if the cards 'work' precisely, that is to say, they answer whatever question we might pose to them accurately, then they do so because we approach the cards from the position of 'all things being equal.' If I get a divorce, when she stops loving me, then I want to know how I can equalize my losses, both emotional and financial. I want to know how I get inspiration from the stars, as it were, so that I may overcome the mess.

When the cards answer my question precisely, they do it because they address both the form and content of my concern. Most people, however, don't make that distinction, and a lot leave the Tarot parlor thinking that the cards have managed to address their particular concern at content level only. 'This is really me the cards have spoken to' many would swear, while thanking the reader profusely for her psychic insights. But I don't get excited.

On my part as a reader, I can see just how the cards address a frame of unity not a fantasy of separation: me against my ex, me against the world, or me against my boss. If the cards give a clear answer related to any of our concerns, it's because they go beyond such mechanisms of identification with identity and whatever clinging to identity brings along. The cards speak accurately not because they are identity-centered but because they are event-centered.

NONDUALISM

This brings me to my second point, the nondual perception, the perception that holds the idea that 'all things being equal' is not about fixing polarity and conflict as part of our efforts, but rather it's about seeing what we call causality as part of unity and presence – for instance, the idea that I'm getting a divorce not because this other thing happened, but because divorce itself is happening (I myself am not married, so I'm not talking about myself here).

Most querents will have a hard time admitting to the reality that things happen simply because they happen and not because something else causes them to happen, and they will cling to making all sorts of identifications that have nothing to do with things happening.

In order to get this, you need to completely suspend your idea of the cards being about you and your situation, and instead see them more as being about events.

Incidentally, however, without these identifications with our conditions and situations – 'I'm in love,' 'I got dumped,' 'my boss hates me' – the fortuneteller would be without a job, but when we talk about the cards addressing our issues precisely, we must allow ourselves a second to contemplate the possibility that the reason why the cards are accurate is not because they have anything to do with us, but because they have a lot to do with us in context, with us being framed by a series of ever changing events.

In this sense we never get to predict the future, as there are no temporal divisions beyond our own constructions and cultural labeling: past, present, and future. What we do when we predict, and what the cards respond to, is operate with an enlarged field of vision ruled by unity not separation. The cards speak the truth accurately because they point to this enlarged field of vision. They are part of it already. The fortuneteller doesn't look into the future; she looks into the expanded field of vision that encompasses the querent's own blind spots, her question, and the reader's interpretation, all happening at the same time.

'But you predicted three months ago that this would happen, and it did happen,' I have clients say to me in awe – which is nice – but I always insist that what I operate with is not belief that this or that will happen, but discovery of how I see this or that happen the moment I read the cards; we conveniently call this 'the future.'

BELIEF AND DISCOVERY

I find the force behind the cards precisely in this distinction between belief and discovery. Many people come to the fortuneteller and think that either they want to or must believe in the cards in order for the cards to 'work.' All the while the cards work because people discover them. People get a glimpse into their own truths, awareness, and expanded fields of vision when they discover the cards *in situ*. That is why the cards work.

The cards work because they are not separate from the questions asked to them. Nor are they separate from the reader interpreting them. The cards work simply because they happen to us. They happen to us exactly at the same time things happen to us.

When we go nodding in approval of what we see, the consistency of what we see as it aligns with our situations, what we nod at is this recognition that things happen to us. When we sit with the cards, we're beyond language and mental constructs. We're in eternity.

THE GOOD TEACHER

In her wonderful book, *The Tarot of Perfection* (2008), Rachel Pollack talks about how the Tarot cards themselves are the teacher, teaching the Tarot reader just what she needs to know. It's not just the Pope who fulfils that function, but all the cards do it. I like this idea. But in the context of 'what is not,' what I also like to entertain as an idea is the fact that, if we want to be even more specific, we could say something like this, borrowing the voice and authority of the Pope: 'You're not a magician when you read the cards. Never think of yourself as a magician when you read the cards, miraculously making the perfect answer appear as if from nowhere. If you're anything, you're a teacher. You teach the other you read the cards for how to speak an entirely new language. This language is not the language of cheap calls. Rather, it's the language that enables you to say what is not.'

At this point, let me bring in another Pope I like, my compatriot and academic colleague, Ioan Couliano, late professor of comparative religion at Chicago University. Here's what he said before the advent of the internet, Instagram, Twitter, and YouTube, in his influential book, *Eros and Magic in the Renaissance* (1984), identifying the magician's con:

> Nowadays, the magician busies himself with public relations, propaganda, market research, sociological surveys, publicity, information, counterinformation and misinformation, censorship, espionage, and even cryptography... (104) Magic is a means of control over the individual and the masses based on deep knowledge of personal and collective erotic impulses. Insofar as science and the manipulation of phantasms are concerned, magic is primarily directed at the human imagination, in which it attempts to create lasting impressions. The magician of the Renaissance is both psychoanalyst and prophet as well as the precursor of modern professions such as director of public relations, propagandist, spy, politician, censor, director of mass communications media, and publicity agent (viii).

Couliano wrote all this in 1984. He anticipated many a horror thing. I see him winking from his grave. Having access to technological innovations, writing platforms, and personal broadcasting 'corporations' does not an authority make. A really good teacher teaches you to speak a language that's even better than the language of the birds, the diviner's language as per 'magical tradition.' The good teacher takes a good look at you, and asks: Are you sure you know who you are? Are your words real? Can you prove it?

THE HANDS AND THE EYES

LET ME CLOSE with this thought. Sometimes you think you're the diviner with the proper clarity. You think that your hands and eyes are the most important. But here's what I say. A good face-to-face divination session starts with paying attention to the following: the hands and the eyes of the sitter. Their strong posture, or lack of it. Their curious gaze.

As for you: always know what you're saying. Be prepared to back up what you're saying with evidence from the cards. Catch the sitters when they are listening, trying to reflect on what you're saying. Stare at them. Don't think it's rude to stare. Quite the contrary. Staring discloses your lucidity, if you have it. If you don't have it, then by all means, use averted gaze, but know that it will not make a strong impression, a strong reading session.

Observe what disturbs, distracts, or attracts. Think of what would happen if you thought of your cartomancy as martial arts. If you were a martial artist, where in the body would your skill sit?

Is your availability to the sitter tenacious? Not all subjects, ailments, and worries grab the heart. You read the cards because you can, not because you think that all lives are glorious, needing nothing but a push of empowerment from you. Miracles don't happen every day, simply because people are not in the habit of thinking about miracles every day. You are what you think, when your thinking is not Zen, of the beyond of 'me-as-culture.'

Think about your hands and your eyes. Is there a difference between them and those of your sitter? This is what I think it's interesting to consider. But what do the cards say?

The Star, the Sun, and the Lovers speak: there's a play of hands here: giving hands, petting hands, snatching hands. Eyes too: in your face, on the water, rolling. 'Oh, you, seducer,' the Lover boy says, clearly referring to the woman on the right, putting his hand on her crotch, her hand on his heart. And yet his eyes are one the other one. What does this mean?

In questions about a love triangle, there's nothing that will please a woman more than to hear that her lover is not that into the other woman. He may have his eyes on her – or is it his hand? – but he's not that into her. Whichever, really, eyes or hands, as long as he's not that into her.

216

What do you make of all this?

Pay attention to what's being poured onto your table. Is comforting appropriate? What's the distance between you and the sitter? You may want to lean in closer, get your head into the other's head, for a true *tête-à-tête*.

Are there any third party hands? Can you identify the influences the sitter is under? Can you go against them? How do you point to your sitter that there's the possibility of too many hands in the deal?

I could go on, but you get the picture. It's plain.

No secret at all.

∞

CITED AND SELECTED WORKS

BRUNNHOLZL, Karl (2016). *The Heart Attack Sutra.* Snow Lion.

CALDWELL, Ross S., Depaulis, Thierry, Ponzi, Marco (2010). *Explaining the Tarot: Two Italian Renaissance Essays on the Meaning of the Tarot Pack.* Maproom Publications.

COULIANO, Ioan (1984). *Eros and Magic in the Renaissance.* University of Chicago Press.

DECKER, Ronald, Depaulis, Thierry, Dummett, Michael, (1996). *A Wicked Pack of Cards: The Origins of the Occult Tarot.* St. Martin's Press.

ELIAS, Camelia, Ed. (2018). *21+1 Fortune-teller's Rules: Read like the Devil Manifestos.* EyeCorner Press.

_____ (2017). *The Power of the Pips. Courting Numbers in Cartomancy.* EyeCorner Press.

_____ (2017). *The Power of the Trumps: A Subtle Burst.* EyeCorner Press.

_____ (2017). 'A Short Cultural History of Divination with the Cards' [https://occult-study.org/a-short-cultural-history-of-divination-with-cards/] Website last accessed on July 27, 2019.

_____ (2015). *The Oracle Travels Light: Principles of Magic with Cards.* EyeCorner Press.

_____ (2014). *Marseille Tarot: Towards the Art of Reading.* EyeCorner Press.

_____ (2015). 'Walking between Worlds: Yeats and the Golden Dawn.' In *Non-Place: Representing Placelessness in Literature, Media and Culture* Eds. Miriam Gebauer et al. Aalborg University Press.

_____ (2013). 'The Wheeling End: Tarot as Eschatological Text.' In *The End: Terminus in Literature, Media and Culture*. Eds. Brian Graham et al. Aalborg University Press.

ENRIQUEZ, Enrique (2011). *Tarology*. EyeCorner Press.

Etteilla (pseudonym of Jean-Baptiste Alliette) (1785). *Manière de se récréer avec le jeu de cartes nomées Tarots*. Paris: Lesclapart.

FARLEY, Helen (2009). *A Cultural History of Tarot: From Entertainment to Esotericism*. I B Tauris & Co Ltd.

GUÉNON, René (2004). *Symbols of Sacred Science*. Sophia Perennis.

HUSON, Paul (2004). *Mystical Origins of the Tarot: From Ancient Roots to Modern Usage*. Destiny Books.

JODOROWSKY, Alejandro (2004). *The Way of Tarot*. Destiny Books.

JOSIPOVICI, Gabriel (1999). *On trust. Art and the Temptations of Suspicion*. Yale University Press.

NISARGADATTA, Maharaj (2012). *I am That*. Trans. Maurice Frydman. The Acron Press.

_____ (1982). *Seeds of Consciousness*. Trans. Jean Dunn. Acron Press.

RIFFATERRE, Michael (1990). *Fictional Truth*. John Hopkins University Press.

POLLACK, Rachel (2008). *The Tarot of Perfection*. Magic Realist Press

SILVESTRE, Colette (1987). *Les Tarots*. Editions Grancher.

SUZUKI, Daizetz (1959). *Zen and the Japanese Culture*. Princeton University Press.

UNGER, Tchalaï (1985). *El Tarot*. Editiones Obelisco.

TATSUMI, Hijikata (2105). *Costume en Face*. Ugly Ducking Press

WAITE, A.E. (1910). *The Pictorial Key to the Tarot*. William Rider & Son.

www.ingramcontent.com/pod-product-compliance
Lightning Source LLC
Chambersburg PA
CBHW061245230426
43662CB00020B/2428